SpringerBriefs in Business

SpringerBriefs present concise summaries of cutting-edge research and practical applications across a wide spectrum of fields. Featuring compact volumes of 50 to 125 pages, the series covers a range of content from professional to academic. Typical topics might include:

- A timely report of state-of-the art analytical techniques
- A bridge between new research results, as published in journal articles, and a contextual literature review
- A snapshot of a hot or emerging topic
- An in-depth case study or clinical example
- A presentation of core concepts that students must understand in order to make independent contributions

SpringerBriefs in Business showcase emerging theory, empirical research, and practical application in management, finance, entrepreneurship, marketing, operations research, and related fields, from a global author community.

Briefs are characterized by fast, global electronic dissemination, standard publishing contracts, standardized manuscript preparation and formatting guidelines, and expedited production schedules.

Svala Gudmundsdottir
Throstur Olaf Sigurjonsson

Sustainability in Banks

A Six-Pillar Model for ESG Integration

Springer

Svala Gudmundsdottir
School of Business
University of Iceland
Reykjavik, Iceland

Throstur Olaf Sigurjonsson
School of Business
University of Iceland
Reykjavik, Iceland

ISSN 2191-5482 ISSN 2191-5490 (electronic)
SpringerBriefs in Business
ISBN 978-3-032-05636-8 ISBN 978-3-032-05637-5 (eBook)
https://doi.org/10.1007/978-3-032-05637-5

This Springer imprint is published by the registered company Springer Nature Switzerland AG
The registered company address is: Gewerbestrasse 11, 6330 Cham, Switzerland

Foreword

In an era of mounting climate risk and rapid financial transformation, the banking sector is at the forefront of shaping a sustainable future. As institutions deeply embedded in society and given their central role in allocating capital and shaping financial flows, banks are uniquely positioned to lead the transition to more responsible and resilient financial systems. Sustainability is no longer an aspirational ideal, it is a strategic and moral imperative.

This book, *Sustainability in Banks: A Six-Pillar Model for ESG Integration*, provides timely insights into how Icelandic banks navigate this complex transformation. It goes beyond surface-level commitments and examines how sustainability is embedded within the architecture of financial institutions. Drawing on qualitative research across four Icelandic banks, it analyzes how internal structures, leadership, regulatory framework and organizational culture intersect to either support or hinder sustainability.

The findings are both contextually grounded and globally relevant. Iceland provides a compelling setting. Small in scale but sophisticated in operation, these institutions function within European regulatory frameworks, reflecting strong national transparency and environmental responsibility. The country's scale also allows for close examination of institutional dynamics, offering lessons for larger and more complex financial systems.

What emerges from this work is a clear message: sustainability should be structurally embedded to be effective. Its placement, whether under strategy, risk, or compliance matters. Structure determines visibility, authority and access to resources. Culture, in turn, shapes whether these structures deliver on their promise.

Icelandic banks lend primarily to companies in industries considered green. Green loans make up 90% of all corporate lending, neutral loans account for 7%, and brown loans for only 3%. The asset allocation of domestic assets held by pension funds is even greener. There, 96% are green assets, 4% are neutral, and there are virtually no brown assets.

This composition benefits not only the environment but also the stability of the financial system. The Central Bank of Iceland's stress tests indicate that, during periods of stress, expected loan losses in brown industries could, on average, be up to three times higher than losses from loans to green industries

This book makes an important contribution to our understanding of institutional change in finance. Let this work inspire dialogue, inform policy and guide the next steps in building a financial system that is resilient, inclusive and accountable to future generations. It is a valuable addition to the ongoing conversation about how institutions can adapt to meet the sustainability imperative at the heart of our shared future.

Minister of Finance and Economic Affairs Daði Már Kristófersson
Reykjavik, Iceland

Acknowledgments

This book would not have been possible without the generous contributions of time, insight, and experience from the individuals we interviewed. The managers and professionals from the Icelandic banking sector shared their perspectives with openness and candor. Their reflections provided a rich foundation for the analysis and made a lasting impact on the direction of the work.

Appreciation is also extended to the academic and institutional environments that supported the development of this research, particularly the resources and flexibility made available for conducting and analyzing the data. Recognition is further due to the broader community of researchers working at the intersection of sustainability, governance, and organizational studies. Their ongoing efforts continue to advance knowledge in this vital area and serve as both inspiration and foundation for the present study. Finally, acknowledgment is given to the personal support systems that sustained the authors throughout the writing process. The encouragement and understanding from those closest to the authors played a quiet yet indispensable role in the completion of this project.

Contents

Contents

Chapter 1
Introduction

Sustainability has emerged as a central concern in the global banking sector, influenced by climate imperatives, regulatory pressure, and evolving stakeholder expectations. Over the past decade, banks have faced increasing scrutiny to generate profits while demonstrating responsibility, transparency, and long-term stewardship of environmental and social capital (Eccles et al., 2014; Edwards et al., 2023). In this context, sustainability has shifted from a peripheral function typically associated with communications or corporate social responsibility (CSR) to a core strategic and operational concern. The global financial sector is undergoing a rapid transformation driven by these sustainability imperatives. Banks are now judged not solely on balance sheets, but on their ability to measure, manage, and report environmental, social, and governance (ESG) performance. Investors demand transparency, regulators require compliance, and employees and customers expect ethical alignment. The critical question is no longer whether sustainability matters, but how it is operationalized within banking institutions (Lozano, 2015; Farr, 2011).

This book examines the organizational positioning of sustainability, exploring where sustainability is situated within banks' internal structures, who is responsible, and how these decisions impact institutional strategy and legitimacy. While many banks publish ESG reports and hire sustainability officers, fewer have effectively integrated sustainability into their decision-making processes. In many cases, sustainability departments begin in communications or human resources (HR) and gradually shift, sometimes unevenly, toward strategy, risk, or finance. These movements are more than cosmetic; they signal whether sustainability is considered a core business or a public relations exercise. Organizational structure is often viewed as a technical concern but also deeply symbolic. The sustainability position within the organizational chart determines access to power, visibility, data, and influence over resource allocation (Galaskiewicz & Wasserman, 1989; Boyle et al., 2021). Sustainability positioned under the CEO's office or within a strategic function signals executive prioritization. By contrast, when sustainability is housed in HR without cross-functional authority, it is more likely to remain marginal.

S. Gudmundsdottir, T. O. Sigurjonsson, *Sustainability in Banks*, SpringerBriefs in Business, https://doi.org/10.1007/978-3-032-05637-5_1

This book approaches structure as both reflective and constitutive of institutional priorities. That is, structure reflects where sustainability stands and actively shapes what it can become. Thornton and Ocasio (1999) argue that institutional logics such as those rooted in risk management, reputational protection, or compliance govern how new practices like ESG integration are interpreted and enacted. Where sustainability is positioned determines which institutional logic it aligns with and how easily it can be integrated into mainstream decision-making.

The core argument of this book is that structural positioning provides a powerful lens for understanding the institutionalization of sustainability in banking. This includes how roles and responsibilities are distributed, how cultural narratives support or undermine sustainability goals, and how structural inertia or reform accelerates or impedes change (Mahoney, 2000).

This study draws on comparative qualitative research conducted within four Icelandic commercial banks. These banks vary in size, ownership, and strategic approach but operate under a shared European regulatory framework and face similar ESG pressures. Iceland provides a valuable context for analysis due to its tightly regulated financial system, strong environmental values, and transparent organizational scale. Its banks are large enough to demonstrate complexity, yet small enough to allow close observation of structural practices.

The empirical foundation of this study is 21 semi-structured interviews with professionals working in sustainability, risk, compliance, project management, operations, and strategic functions across the four case banks. The interviews explored how sustainability was organized, who was involved, and how internal roles and responsibilities evolved in response to external ESG expectations and regulatory developments. Across the interviews, several recurring themes emerged. In most banks, sustainability initiatives began as symbolic or voluntary efforts, often managed by communications or human resources. Over time and typically prompted by either regulatory pressure or strong internal champions, these functions gradually moved toward the institution's core, particularly into risk and finance units. This journey from symbolism to substance was often slow, contested, and uneven, revealing the institutional resistance that sustainability professionals frequently encountered. Regulation played a critical, though double-edged, role. On one hand, regulatory frameworks such as the Sustainable Finance Disclosure Regulation (SFDR) and the Corporate Sustainability Reporting Directive (CSRD) brought new legitimacy and urgency to sustainability efforts. On the other hand, these frameworks introduced significant complexity, administrative burden, and compliance fatigue. Some banks responded with narrow disclosure-focused strategies, while others used regulation as a strategic lever for broader integration.

At the same time, the interviews underscored that structural location alone did not determine success. Even when sustainability was formally positioned in strategic or risk-related departments, outcomes varied dramatically. Organizational culture, defined by how people think, speak, and behave to sustainability, plays a pivotal role. Banks with open, learning-oriented cultures were more likely to integrate sustainability into their day-to-day practices. Conversely, in institutions with rigid hierarchies or conservative risk postures, ESG initiatives often remained isolated from core decision-making processes (Christensen et al., 2013; De Smet et al., 2021).

Another insight was the growing importance of project management for operationalizing sustainability. Banks increasingly rely on cross-functional project teams, pilot initiatives, and agile methodologies to translate high-level ESG goals into actionable steps. The role of Project Management Offices (PMOs), change managers, and internal sustainability "champions" became essential in coordinating efforts across departments and tracking progress over time. Finally, banks wrestled with the tension between centralizing sustainability expertise and distributing ESG responsibilities across business lines. Some created dedicated ESG units with broad mandates, while others embedded sustainability coordinators within each operational division. Each model had trade-offs; centralized units ensured consistency and oversight, while distributed models encouraged ownership and contextual relevance. Balancing these dynamics was an ongoing organizational challenge. These themes are explored across the chapters of this book and are not limited to the Icelandic context. They reflect broader dynamics in European and global banking systems, particularly as ESG expectations become institutionalized in financial regulations and investor practices (Lozano, 2015; Eccles et al., 2014).

This book contributes to sustainability scholarship by focusing on the internal organizational dimensions of ESG integration. This area has received less attention than policy analysis, ESG performance ratings, or external reporting studies. The book presents a more grounded view of institutional transformation by examining how sustainability is structurally embedded and how this structure interacts with leadership, culture, and systems. For practitioners, the study offers insight into what makes sustainability integration effective in real terms, visibility, alignment, strategic fit, and internal coherence. For regulators and policymakers, the book demonstrates how external mandates influence internal decision-making processes and how regulation can unintentionally shape or hinder sustainability progress, depending on internal structures. In essence, sustainability in banking encompasses not only strategy and performance but also design. How banks organize themselves around ESG priorities is a strong signal of their values and strategic intent. Sustainability must be treated as a structural issue, not a cosmetic one; thoughtful architecture, clear roles, and a supportive culture are essential to its integration.

This introductory chapter establishes the study's motivation, scope, and methodology. The following chapters offer a detailed analysis of sustainability structures, coordination mechanisms, cultural dynamics, project-based integration, and regulatory responses across the four case banks.

1.1 Concluding Remarks

In conclusion, this chapter has established the conceptual and empirical foundations of the book. It has been argued that the structural positioning of sustainability within banks is a critical but often overlooked factor in shaping how ESG commitments are interpreted, implemented, and institutionalized. By drawing on the experiences of four Icelandic banks and focusing on internal organizational arrangements, the book aims to deepen our understanding of what makes sustainability integration effective in practice. Proceeding to the next chapter, the analysis focuses on the specific structural choices of banks, the organization of departments, the location of sustainability functions, and what these configurations reveal about institutional priorities. Through this exploration, the book contributes to the academic literature and the practical work of transforming banking into a more sustainable and accountable sector.

References

Boyle, M., Goswin, K., & Higgis, M. A. (2021). *Organizational transformation: How to achieve it and what to avoid*. Middle Tennessee State University.

Christensen, L. T., Morsing, M., & Thyssen, O. (2013). CSR as aspirational talk. *Organization, 20*(3), 372–393. https://doi.org/10.1177/1350508413478310

De Smet A., Gao W., Henderson K., & Hundertmark T. (2021). *Organizing for sustainability success: Where, and how, leaders can start | McKinsey*. Retrieved February 23, 2025, from https://www.mckinsey.com/capabilities/sustainability/our-insights/organizingfor-sustainability-success-where-and-how-leaders-can-start

Eccles, R. G., Ioannou, I., & Serafeim, G. (2014). The impact of corporate sustainability on organizational processes and performance. *Management Science, 60*(11), 2835–2857. https://doi.org/10.1287/mnsc.2014.1984

Edwards, W., Jain, R., Soehner, C., Nadeau, M. -C., & og Stephens, D. (2023). Green growth: Unlocking sustainability opportunities for retail banks. McKinsey Sustainability. https://www.mckinsey.com/capabilities/sustainability/ourinsights/green-growth-unlocking-sustainability-opportunities-for-retail-banks

Farr, H. J. (2011, July 28). *Organizational structure for sustainability*. Blue Cross Blue Shield of Massachusetts. EDF Climate Corps.

Galaskiewicz, J., & Wasserman, S. (1989). Mimetic processes within an interorganizational field: An empirical test. *Administrative Science Quarterly, 34*(3), 454–479. https://doi.org/10.2307/2393153

Lozano, R. (2015). A holistic perspective on corporate sustainability drivers. *Corporate Social Responsibility and Environmental Management, 22*(1), 32–44. https://doi.org/10.1002/csr.1325

Mahoney, J. (2000). Path dependence in historical sociology. *Theory and Society, 29*(4), 507–548. https://doi.org/10.1023/A:1007113830879

Thornton, P. H., & Ocasio, W. (1999). Institutional logics and the historical contingency of power in organizations: Executive succession in the higher education publishing industry, 1958–1990. *American Journal of Sociology, 105*(3), 801–843. https://doi.org/10.1086/210361

Chapter 2
Organizational Structures and the Location of Sustainability

2.1 Chapter Content

The organizational structure of a bank is more than an administrative framework it is a blueprint of authority, priorities, and power. Where sustainability is positioned within that framework significantly shapes how it is perceived, resourced, and enacted. This chapter examines how different structural arrangements across four Icelandic banks influence the integration of sustainability principles into organizational routines, strategy, and culture. Drawing on insights from interviews and theoretical framing, the chapter examines how structure interacts with institutional logic, leadership commitment, and operational complexity.

Sustainability initiatives are often launched in response to growing external pressure from regulators, investors, customers, and civil society. However, whether these initiatives lead to substantive change depends largely on internal decisions, particularly how roles are defined, departments are configured, and reporting lines are established. As Galaskiewicz and Wasserman (1989) argue, formal structure serves as a means of both internally and externally communicating institutional intent. Sustainability, when structurally marginalized, is easily perceived as peripheral or symbolic. Conversely, when embedded in strategic functions, it gains influence and coherence.

The Icelandic banks examined in this study displayed a variety of structural arrangements. In Bank A, sustainability was positioned under the CEO's office and supported by a cross-functional council reporting to the executive board. This centralization granted visibility and authority but required constant coordination with business units. In Bank B, sustainability had evolved from being a marketing-driven initiative to a risk-driven agenda, now embedded in the compliance division. Bank C followed a decentralized approach, with sustainability responsibilities dispersed across departments. Finally, Bank D established a standalone sustainability department with a dotted-line reporting structure to strategy and a formal reporting line to

S. Gudmundsdottir, T. O. Sigurjonsson, *Sustainability in Banks*, SpringerBriefs in Business, https://doi.org/10.1007/978-3-032-05637-5_2

the board. Each model offers distinct advantages and trade-offs. As seen in Bank A, centralized structures ensure strategic alignment and allow for more unified reporting and policy coherence as suggested by Lozano (2015). However, they risk creating silos if not well integrated into operational processes. Decentralized models, like Bank C's, encourage departmental ownership and responsiveness but may lead to inconsistencies and coordination challenges. One sustainability officer from Bank C noted, "Each department is doing something, but we're not always pulling in the same direction."

Structural choices also reflect and reinforce broader institutional logics. Thornton and Ocasio (1999) describe institutional logics as socially constructed patterns of cultural symbols and material practices. In banks, these logics often revolve around risk, profitability, compliance, and reputation. The location of sustainability in relation to these dominant logics influences its perceived relevance. For example, placing ESG under risk aligns it with a logic of prudence and protection. Placing it under communications aligns it with a logic of branding and legitimacy. Interviewees reported that these associations had tangible consequences for influence and resourcing.

This movement, often referred to as the migration of sustainability, is frequently nonlinear. In several banks, sustainability functions have been relocated multiple times in recent years. Regulatory changes, leadership transitions, or internal restructuring were the primary drivers of these shifts. The Sustainable Finance Disclosure Regulation (SFDR) and Corporate Sustainability Reporting Directive (CSRD), for instance, prompted some banks to relocate ESG responsibilities closer to finance and risk to ensure accurate reporting and risk assessment alignment (Eccles et al., 2014). In Bank D, a newly appointed board member with a background in climate finance pushed for creating a dedicated ESG department and elevated its reporting line. Professional background also shapes structure. In the early stages, sustainability teams often emerge from communications or human resources, focusing on stakeholder engagement or internal culture (Christensen et al., 2013). As data and regulatory demands increased, banks began hiring professionals with expertise in environmental science, data analytics, or financial risk. This shift in competencies necessitated new structures that enabled access to core systems, financial data, and credit portfolios. One executive described the change as "moving from storytelling to systems thinking."

Several banks in the study experimented with hybrid models, combining central coordination with embedded ESG roles across departments. Bank A established a sustainability office with strategic oversight, assigning ESG focal points to key areas, including lending, procurement, and IT. This matrix structure supported flexibility but required continuous negotiation of roles and accountability. One manager noted, "It works well when the people are committed. However, when priorities shift, it can unravel quickly." Coordination mechanisms play a crucial role in making these structures effective. ESG steering groups, sustainability committees, and informal task forces commonly align goals across business units. Bank B established an ESG task force, chaired by the CFO, which comprised representatives from strategy, operations, legal, and sustainability. This task force met monthly as a cross-functional decision-making body, helping resolve bottlenecks and clarify overlapping responsibilities. However, such mechanisms require sustained attention and follow-through. One participant noted, "Committees help us communicate with each other, but they only work if people view them as decision-making arenas, not just as a means of providing updates."

Banks also rely on informal brokers, with credibility and access, who connect siloed departments and facilitate cross-functional collaboration. These sustainability "champions" serve a crucial bridging role, translating broad ESG goals into actionable terms at the operational level. Though their efforts often go unnoticed, they are vital to embedding sustainability within daily practices. At Bank C, for example, a sustainability coordinator described spending much of her time "walking the halls," cultivating relationships, and sharing best practices. These informal roles, while challenging to institutionalize, function as the connective tissue between organizational structures and actual execution. However, even with such internal champions, banks often face structural inertia. Organizational arrangements, once established, tend to resist adaptation even when strategic direction shifts. This form of path dependency (Mahoney, 2000) can lead to outdated reporting lines and inefficient allocation of responsibilities. One interviewee illustrated this disconnect, noting that her department remained aligned with a legacy division that had little relevance to ESG, despite a strong push from leadership for sustainability integration. "We've changed our mission, but not our map," she observed, underscoring how structural lag can dampen momentum and send mixed signals about the institution's true level of commitment.

This issue of structural positioning is closely tied to the allocation of resources. Banks that embed sustainability within core functions, such as risk or finance, or where ESG initiatives report directly to senior executives, tend to provide these teams with greater access to funding, data infrastructure, and cross-unit collaboration. By contrast, when ESG functions are situated at the organizational periphery, they often face staffing shortages, ambiguous mandates, and reliance on more powerful departments to gain visibility. Interviewees from such contexts described spending considerable energy "advocating for inclusion" in internal decision-making processes, further highlighting how structure shapes capability and legitimacy. Structural clarity is also essential for external communication. Investors and regulators are increasingly scrutinizing governance arrangements related to environmental, social, and governance (ESG) sustainability. Banks that can demonstrate internal alignment, with clear roles and reporting pathways, are more likely to be seen as credible. One compliance officer emphasized, "Structure is part of our story. If we can't explain how we're organized, it's hard to show that we're serious."

Technology and information systems influence structural coherence. Banks with ESG data platforms and integrated dashboards can better coordinate efforts across units. Those relying on disconnected systems face duplication and miscommunication. Several interviewees emphasized the importance of systems that accurately reflect their underlying structural intentions. "Structure without tools is just a diagram," said one compliance officer. "We need systems that make the structure work." Leadership emerged as a key enabler or constraint. The structure followed suit in banks where the CEO or board championed sustainability. In others, ESG remained at mid-management level, vulnerable to turnover or shifting strategic focus. Leadership signaling through public statements, resource allocation, and committee involvement was seen as essential for giving structural reforms staying power. A director at Bank D explained, "We created the department, but it only got traction when the CEO started using the word 'climate' in strategy meetings."

Organizational learning played a crucial role in the structural evolution. Banks with feedback loops, learning sessions, and after-action reviews were more likely to adapt their structures over time. In Bank A, quarterly ESG learning reviews included representatives from legal, credit, operations, and sustainability, helping to identify blind spots and share innovations. This iterative approach enabled the structure to evolve in tandem with the goals and capacities suggested by Lozano (2015). Cultural alignment also remained a critical factor. Even well-designed structures struggled in cultures that resisted change or viewed sustainability as secondary. Interviewees in Bank C described a disconnect between formal ESG goals and day-to-day decision-making. "We have the charts, we have the roles, but culturally, it's still not embedded," one said. Banks that succeeded in aligning structure and culture often relied on storytelling, peer-to-peer training, and leadership modeling. Finally, benchmarking structural practices against peer institutions supported internal legitimacy. Icelandic banks frequently referenced Nordic and European counterparts as inspiration. One interviewee from Bank B described attending international working groups to understand how others incorporated ESG into their governance. "It helps us make the case internally," she said. "If others are putting sustainability at risk, or linking it to finance, we can say, 'This isn't just an idea, it's the direction the sector is moving.'"

2.2 Concluding Remarks

The organizational positioning of sustainability is a critical determinant of its influence and impact. This chapter has demonstrated how structure affects the location of sustainability and its functioning within the broader framework of the bank. Through comparative analysis and interview data, the distinct pathways provided by centralized, decentralized, and hybrid models, each shaped by institutional logic, leadership support, cultural alignment, and technological infrastructure, have been assessed.

There is no universally optimal model, but there are common enablers: visible leadership, strategic alignment, resourced teams, cross-functional collaboration, and systems that reinforce formal structures. As sustainability grows in strategic significance, banks must treat structural design not as an afterthought but as a lever for transformation. When combined with culture and governance, structure becomes not just a map of roles but a roadmap for change.

References

Christensen, L. T., Morsing, M., & Thyssen, O. (2013). CSR as aspirational talk. *Organization, 20*(3), 372–393.

Eccles, R. G., Ioannou, I., & Serafeim, G. (2014). The impact of corporate sustainability on organizational processes and performance. *Management Science, 60*(11), 2835–2857.

Galaskiewicz, J., & Wasserman, S. (1989). Mimetic processes within an inter-organizational field: An empirical test. *Administrative Science Quarterly, 34*(3), 454–479.

Lozano, R. (2015). A holistic perspective on corporate sustainability drivers. *Corporate Social Responsibility and Environmental Management, 22*(1), 32–44.

Mahoney, J. (2000). Path dependence in historical sociology. *Theory and Society, 29*(4), 507–548.

Thornton, P. H., & Ocasio, W. (1999). Institutional logic and the historical contingency of power in organizations. *American Journal of Sociology, 105*(3), 801–843.

Chapter 3
Governance, Committees, and the Role of Leadership

3.1 Chapter Content

To further expand the understanding of governance and sustainability in banks, the interplay between sustainability governance and corporate governance codes is examined, with a focus on cross-sectoral comparisons and the influence of national regulatory cultures. Moreover, emerging perspectives from behavioral governance and systems thinking can add nuance to current models. Corporate governance codes in many jurisdictions increasingly emphasize the importance of sustainability oversight. The revised Shareholder Rights Directive and Corporate Sustainability Reporting Directive (CSRD) mandate greater board responsibility for ESG issues in Europe. These reforms prompt banks to expand traditional governance beyond financial performance, requiring boards to establish sustainability objectives and monitor relevant performance indicators (Bruno & Lagasio, 2021). The introduction of double materiality in the CSRD represents a paradigm shift, banks must account not only for sustainability risks to the institution but also the institution's impact on society and the environment. National regulatory culture also plays a crucial role. Icelandic banks are influenced not only by EU frameworks but also by domestic traditions of social responsibility and strong state involvement in the financial sector following the 2008 crisis. This creates both opportunities and tensions. On the one hand, there is institutional receptiveness to reform; on the other hand, there is inertia from legacy governance structures. One interviewee noted that while sustainability rhetoric had increased, "old habits in committee dynamics die hard." Cultural embeddedness, therefore, influences the rate at which governance reforms are adopted (Jerónimo et al., 2020).

Comparative governance studies show that banks in the Nordics often outperform their peers in integrating sustainability. This can be attributed to stronger

S. Gudmundsdottir, T. O. Sigurjonsson, *Sustainability in Banks*, SpringerBriefs in Business, https://doi.org/10.1007/978-3-032-05637-5_3

stakeholder orientation, collaborative organizational cultures, and progressive corporate governance codes. For example, Scandinavian banks often incorporate ESG considerations into their supervisory board discussions and annual reports. By contrast, banks in more shareholder-centric systems may lag in adopting substantive sustainability governance, relying instead on voluntary guidelines or reputational incentives (Lozano & Garcia, 2020). A cross-sectoral lens adds further value. Governance innovations in other sectors, such as healthcare and energy, demonstrate how integrated reporting, stakeholder engagement through panels, and real-time audit trails can enhance ESG accountability. For instance, hospitals using stakeholder councils to advise on social equity issues have demonstrated measurable improvements in patient outcomes and community trust. Banks could adapt similar approaches by establishing standing ESG panels or rotating stakeholder forums to democratize input into governance (Ioannou, 2019).

Behavioral governance theories provide additional insight. Rather than viewing boards and committees as purely rational actors, these theories consider the cognitive biases, heuristics, and group dynamics that shape governance behavior. For instance, "ESG inertia" can occur when dominant voices in committees marginalize dissent or when confirmation bias leads to an underestimation of long-term risks. Encouraging diversity of thought, structured dissent, and external facilitation can mitigate such effects (Schein, 2004). Systems thinking can also reframe sustainability governance. Rather than isolated decisions by discrete bodies, it views governance as a system of interrelated feedback loops. A change in board composition influences executive hiring, shaping cultural norms and ultimately affecting frontline decision-making. From this perspective, effective sustainability governance requires aligning multiple nodes, boards, management, departments, and data systems into a coherent strategy. Disruption or misalignment at any point weakens the whole system (Silvius, 2021).

Interviewees stressed the importance of learning from failure. In one instance, a bank launched a sustainability strategy without involving its risk and compliance teams early. The result was a misalignment between sustainability targets and risk appetite, leading to internal confusion and delayed implementation. This highlights the importance of integrated planning, where sustainability initiatives are rigorously tested against institutional risk frameworks from the outset (Central Bank of Iceland, 2024). Ultimately, ESG governance is increasingly intertwined with digital transformation. Artificial intelligence, blockchain, and big data analytics are being explored to enhance ESG reporting and decision-making. Some banks experiment with AI-driven dashboards that flag potential ESG risks in real time or automate impact assessment reports. These tools can reduce manual reporting burdens and improve the granularity of oversight, provided they are ethically governed and integrated with human judgment (IcelandSIF, n.d.-b).

As banks navigate a shifting sustainability landscape, the need for reflexive and forward-looking governance becomes increasingly urgent. Embedding ESG into board agendas, incentivizing innovation, fostering behavioral and cognitive diversity, and integrating technology will distinguish leaders from laggards. In this sense, sustainability governance is not just a structural issue but a strategic and cultural imperative for banks committed to long-term value creation. The governance structures that underpin sustainability work in banks are critical to ensuring that environmental and social objectives are not merely rhetorical but embedded in everyday decision-making. These structures determine who is responsible for sustainability and how decisions are made, who has a seat at the table, and how effectively the institution responds to new demands. Governance arrangements for sustainability vary significantly among the case banks. Some institutions have formal sustainability committees chaired by CEOs or other C-level executives, while others rely on informal networks or subcommittees within broader risk or compliance functions. The evolution of these committees often reflects strategic shifts. For example, in Bank A, sustainability was initially housed in the communications department before becoming a board-level priority, signifying a cultural and structural elevation of its importance (Financial Supervisory Authority, 2022).

A common theme among interviewees was the importance of leadership involvement. In Bank C, the CEO's active participation in sustainability committee meetings was critical in aligning organizational culture with sustainability objectives. One interviewee noted, "When the CEO attends, everyone listens." This top-level engagement communicates that sustainability is not a peripheral issue, but a central strategic concern (De Smet et al., 2021). Nevertheless, the presence of formal structures does not guarantee effectiveness. Though well-defined on paper, some committees lacked operational authority or integration with business lines. This "symbolic governance" can satisfy external pressures without fostering genuine change (Sideri, 2021). The need for symbolic governance to evolve into substantive governance, where decisions result in tangible resources, actionable steps, and measurable outcomes has therefore been argued and suggested by Eccles & Serafeim (2013). Stakeholder theory contextualizes this complexity. Banks operate within a multilayered environment comprising regulators, investors, customers, and the public. Committees are platforms to reconcile these often-conflicting demands (Warner-Søderholm et al., 2024). However, their legitimacy hinges on executive backing and alignment with internal strategies. Committee composition significantly impacts sustainability integration. When representatives from core business units, such as lending or risk management, are involved, sustainability principles have a significant impact on financial products and credit policies. In contrast, committees limited to staff functions such as HR or communications struggle to gain traction in strategic decision-making (Krisciukaityte et al., 2023).

Bank B exemplifies a highly formalized governance model, characterized by well-documented ESG roles, regular meetings, and clear key performance indicators (KPIs). This approach fosters accountability and allows progress tracking (Central Bank of Iceland, 2024). Bank D, however, favored informal coordination via working groups. While more flexible, this approach risked inconsistency and lacked clarity in responsibilities. Agile governance emerged in Bank C's creation of a cross-functional task force to develop a green bond strategy. Led on a rotating basis and involving staff from various units, this task force quickly mobilized organizational knowledge and resources. Its success stemmed from the principles of decentralization, collaboration, and iterative learning emphasized in agile frameworks. Several interviewees highlighted persistent barriers, including misalignment between ESG and financial priorities, inadequate data infrastructure, and a lack of ESG expertise. Some banks introduced ESG training programs for executives and board members to bridge this gap, helping translate technical standards into strategic insights. Organizational learning plays a pivotal role. Banks that embed ESG into balanced scorecards, strategic reviews, and internal audits are known to show greater coherence and momentum. Further, when executive compensation is linked to sustainability outcomes, it reinforces long-term alignment (Bossidy et al., 2002; Lozano & Garcia, 2020).

Hybrid governance models, which combine centralized oversight with decentralized action units, offer a promising balance. While central committees ensured consistency, distributed teams tailored sustainability actions to local contexts. This dual model enhanced accountability and peer learning as suggeted by Ioannou (2019). Governance extended beyond internal structures. Some banks have established external advisory boards comprising representatives from NGOs and academics to review and co-create their ESG strategies. This participatory model considered to have elevated transparency and public trust (Nasdaq, 2020). Digitalization was another trend. Dashboards displaying real-time ESG metrics enabled more informed and timely decision-making. However, technological disparities among banks created uneven governance capacity (IcelandSIF, n.d.). Relational dynamics also matter. Committees that foster psychological safety, open dialogue, and mutual respect are known to be more effective than those mired in rigid hierarchies or political posturing (Schein, 2004; Jerónimo et al., 2020). Middle managers can serve as a bridge between strategy and implementation. Their engagement in governance processes are vital to operationalizing ESG strategies. When empowered and well-informed, they can become crucial agents of change (Lozano & Garcia, 2020). Innovation governance was another evolution. Some committees actively supported experimental projects, such as green fintech tools or sustainable investment products, requiring members with expertise in innovation and a risk-tolerant mindset (Simard & Aubry, 2024). Integrating ESG with broader risk management systems emerged as a best practice. Banks aligned ESG taxonomies with EU standards (e.g., SFDR, EU Taxonomy), enabling consistent, compliant, and efficient risk assessments (Central Bank of Iceland, 2024). Transparency remained paramount. Publishing mandates, decision logs, and outcomes elevated credibility and stakeholder confidence. Effective governance is visible, not hidden behind internal bureaucracy (De Smet et al., 2021). Lastly, the role of the Project Management Office (PMO) was emphasized. PMOs helped standardize sustainability initiatives, monitor risks, and manage complex, cross-departmental ESG projects. Their inclusion in governance structures signaled a commitment to execution, not just planning (Silvius, 2021; Institute Project Management, 2022).

3.2 Concluding Remarks

This chapter demonstrates that effective sustainability governance in banks is neither static nor one-size-fits-all. Instead, it emerges from a dynamic alignment of purpose, power, and practice across diverse institutional contexts. The interviews and cases reveal how leadership engagement, committee structures, digital tools, and organizational culture collectively shape the execution of ESG objectives. Where these elements reinforce each other, sustainability is more likely to transition from a symbolic aspiration to a strategic priority. Crucially, the role of the CEO and senior leadership cannot be overstated. Their visible commitment legitimizes ESG within the organization and ensures alignment between strategy, operations, and accountability mechanisms. Committees and governance structures play a central role; however, their influence depends on their integration with core business units, clarity in their mandates, and responsiveness to internal and external feedback. As banks face intensifying ESG disclosure requirements, stakeholder expectations, and climate-related risks, governance must evolve to meet these demands. Future-ready governance systems are agile, inclusive, and digitally enabled. They institutionalize learning, foster collaboration, and link ESG performance to strategic decision-making. Ultimately, sustainability governance is not just a matter of structure; it is a reflection of organizational will, leadership vision, and institutional maturity. The banks that lead in this space do so by embedding sustainability into the very architecture of governance, ensuring that ESG is not an add-on but a core lens through which value is created and decisions are made.

References

Bossidy, L., Charan, R., & Burck, C. (2002). *Execution: The discipline of getting things done*. Crown Business.

Bruno, A., & Lagasio, V. (2021). Corporate governance and sustainability disclosure: Evidence from the European banking sector. *Sustainability, 13*(11), 6160. https://doi.org/10.3390/su13116160

Central Bank of Iceland. (2024). *Sustainability and risk reports*.

De Smet, A., Mysore, M., & Meshkinpour, A. (2021). *Organizational culture: From old habits to new behavior*. McKinsey & Company. https://www.mckinsey.com/business-functions/people-and-organizational-performance/our-insights/organizational-culture-from-old-habits-to-new-behavior

Eccles, R. G., & Serafeim, G. (2013). The performance frontier: Innovating for a sustainable strategy. *Harvard Business Review, 91*(5), 50–60.

Financial Supervisory Authority. (2022). *ESG risk guidelines for financial institutions*.

IcelandSIF. (n.d.). *Sustainable finance and investment tools: Reports and dashboards*.

Institute Project Management. (2022). ESG and project governance standards.

Ioannou, I. (2019). *Redefining the purpose of the corporation*. London Business School Review.

Jerónimo, H. M., Arrau, P. A., & Martinho, C. (2020). Enhancing sustainability through organizational culture: A multiple case study. *Journal of Cleaner Production, 275*, 122944. https://doi.org/10.1016/j.jclepro.2020.122944

Krisciukaityte, R., Eidukaitė, A., & Leitonienė, S. (2023). ESG integration in banking: Perspectives from the Baltics. *Baltic Journal of Economics, 23*(1), 65–82. https://doi.org/10.1080/1406099X.2023.2167511

Lozano, R., & Garcia, R. (2020). Achieving corporate sustainability through organizational learning. *Journal of Cleaner Production, 258*, 120613. https://doi.org/10.1016/j.jclepro.2020.120613

Nasdaq. (2020). *ESG reporting guide for European companies*.

Schein, E. H. (2004). *Organizational culture and leadership* (3rd ed.). Jossey-Bass.

Sideri, A. (2021). Symbolic management and sustainability: The illusion of green governance. *Environmental Policy and Governance, 31*(3), 234–245. https://doi.org/10.1002/eet.1923

Silvius, G. (2021). Sustainability in project management: A literature review and impact analysis. *Procedia Computer Science, 181*, 137–144. https://doi.org/10.1016/j.procs.2021.01.123

Simard, M., & Aubry, M. (2024). Innovation in sustainability governance: Role of project managers. *Project Management Journal*.

Warner-Søderholm, G., et al. (2024). Sustainable leadership in financial services. *Nordic Journal of Business, 73*(1), 24–49.

Chapter 4
Roles and Tasks: Specialists, Committees, and Managers

4.1 Chapter Content

Sustainability specialists play a crucial role in anchoring institutional knowledge and ensuring compliance with evolving standards, such as the Corporate Sustainability Reporting Directive (CSRD) and the Sustainable Finance Disclosure Regulation (SFDR). However, interviewees frequently described feelings of role overload. These professionals often manage sustainability reporting, support strategic planning, coordinate with auditors and consultants, and serve as internal advisors. Their work involves constant negotiation between long-term goals and short-term deliverables, formal authority and informal influence, and between high expectations and modest resources (Lozano & Garcia, 2020). A significant theme in the data was the symbolic placement of sustainability functions. While most teams were formally affiliated with senior leadership (e.g., under the CEO's office or strategy divisions), they were not always empowered to influence decisions. This symbolic positioning, characterized by visibility but not authority, necessitated that sustainability professionals rely on persuasive skills rather than formal power (Sideri, 2021). This aligns with prior research suggesting that sustainability leadership often depends on soft influence, storytelling, and strategic networking rather than hierarchical control (Eccles & Serafeim, 2013).

Committees played a key role in linking specialist roles with operational functions. In well-performing cases, sustainability committees were structured to include representatives from finance, risk, operations, HR, and even product development. This created pathways for information flow and joint decision-making. However, where committees lacked clear charters, regular meetings, or KPIs, they were often described as "talk shops" forums for discussion rather than levers for action (Simard & Aubry, 2024). Cross-functional initiatives showed particular promise. In Bank B, a task force involving sustainability staff, IT, and retail banking units developed an internal dashboard to track ESG performance metrics. This collaboration enhanced

S. Gudmundsdottir, T. O. Sigurjonsson, *Sustainability in Banks*, SpringerBriefs in Business, https://doi.org/10.1007/978-3-032-05637-5_4

data access, enabling departments to take ownership of their contributions. It also strengthened the status of sustainability staff as knowledge brokers and systems integrators, as suggested by Silvius (2021).

Professional backgrounds were highly diverse across banks. Specialists came from various fields, including environmental sciences, law, business, and communications. This diversity reflected the interdisciplinary nature of sustainability work but also produced tensions. For instance, staff with environmental backgrounds sometimes struggled to understand internal budgeting cycles or regulatory framing. In contrast, business-oriented staff faced challenges translating technical ESG data into meaningful insights as suggested by Jerónimo et al. (2020). As a result, the most effective teams balance complementary skill sets, with hiring increasingly favoring hybrid profiles. A related finding concerned career development. Interviewees highlighted the limited upward mobility opportunities in sustainability roles in all four banks. Most positions lacked formal career ladders or pathways into leadership. This stagnation discouraged talent retention and sometimes sent implicit signals that ESG work was not part of the bank's core mission. Banks that began linking sustainability experience to leadership training or rotational programs appeared better positioned to retain talent and grow internal capacity (Bruno & Lagasio, 2021).

Training programs for middle managers were seen as essential. While senior leaders often endorsed sustainability in principle, implementation depended on buy-in from mid-level staff. Nevertheless, few banks had systematic programs for embedding ESG competencies into leadership development or operational onboarding. This lack of training led to role ambiguity, where managers were expected to act on sustainability goals without understanding how these goals fit within their performance frameworks. Another promising model was using sustainability "ambassadors" or "champions" across departments. These individuals, often volunteers or semi-formal appointees, acted as points of contact for the central sustainability team. Their success depended heavily on institutional support: time allocation, recognition, and training. When well-supported, these champions expanded awareness and fostered peer learning. When poorly supported, they reported frustration and role confusion.

The emotional dimensions of sustainability work also emerged strongly in interviews. Specialists spoke of passion, frustration, burnout, and isolation. One noted, "People assume you're idealistic, but this is also just very hard work." Another said, "I spend more time convincing people than doing the actual work." This emotional labor, exacerbated by ambiguity and under-resourcing, should be taken into account in staffing plans, well-being programs, and performance evaluations.

In this context, technological tools are not just operational aids but also crucial supports that can alleviate some of the emotional and cognitive load that sustainability professionals bear. Manual data collection, often conducted through spreadsheets and email, remains a common practice but is often insufficient. Banks that invested in ESG software platforms, workflow integration, and digital reporting systems were better able to track progress and reduce reliance on overburdened staff. Moreover, linking sustainability tools with financial planning systems increase the perceived relevance of ESG metrics (IcelandSIF, n.d.).

An emerging trend is the integration of sustainability into project management offices (PMOs). In Bank D, sustainability professionals were embedded into PMOs responsible for major IT and infrastructure upgrades. This ensured ESG risks and opportunities were assessed early in the project lifecycle. It also elevated the status of sustainability staff, aligning their work with high-visibility initiatives (Institute Project Management, 2022). Building on this integration, some banks adopted dual-reporting structures to enhance department collaboration. In these models, sustainability professionals maintained a functional line to the central ESG team while reporting operationally to business unit heads. While this improved alignment, it also created ambiguity around accountability and performance. Clear role definitions, shared evaluation criteria, and ongoing dialogue were essential to making such structures work as suggested by Lozano & Garcia (2020). Beyond internal arrangements, external actors have also played a significant role in shaping the structure of sustainability within banks. Pressure from investors, regulators, and civil society helped legitimize internal sustainability roles. In one instance, a bank created a new ESG analyst position in response to a shareholder engagement that highlighted reporting gaps. In another instance, NGOs pushed for greater transparency and accountability in environmental lending, prompting internal reorganization. These examples demonstrate how external advocacy can influence internal task structures and enhance the visibility of sustainability work (UNEP FI, 2019).

To further enrich this chapter and provide a broader perspective, examining how sustainability roles in Icelandic banks compare to international benchmarks is valuable. Globally, banks are increasingly integrating Environmental, Social, and Governance (ESG) considerations into their core structures. In European markets such as Germany and the Netherlands, sustainability positions are often embedded directly in credit risk and compliance functions, indicating a higher degree of operational integration than is typical in Iceland (Bruno & Lagasio, 2021). Research also highlights the trend of professionalizing ESG roles. In leading institutions, ESG professionals are not generalists but possess certifications in sustainability reporting, climate risk, or sustainable finance (Ioannou & Serafeim, 2019). This contrasts with the Icelandic model, where ESG responsibilities often fall to enthusiastic but overburdened staff with diverse and sometimes mismatched academic backgrounds. Professionalization through formal qualification frameworks, partnerships with universities, and recognition within HR systems can help elevate ESG roles, attract top talent, and support employee retention. Cross-sector insights offer further lessons. In the energy sector, for instance, many organizations have created dual-career paths that reward technical ESG expertise without requiring a shift into general management. Adapting this model could allow banks to retain skilled ESG professionals who may not wish to move into unrelated leadership roles (Silvius, 2021).

There is also a growing trend toward using artificial intelligence (AI) and machine learning (ML) in sustainability management. Some large banks and asset managers are leveraging AI to scan portfolios for climate-related risk exposures, flag social media sentiment on ESG controversies, and automatically generate compliance reports. Although Icelandic banks are still in the early stages of this digital transition, interviewees expressed interest in technologies that can reduce administrative burdens and enhance analytical capabilities. Successful integration, however, depends on cross-training between sustainability and data science teams, as well as strong data governance protocols (Tan & Tsionas, 2022). Training programs deserve renewed attention. Many banks in the study had basic ESG onboarding modules, but few had advanced or role-specific training paths. In contrast, leading European banks such as ING and Nordea have launched comprehensive ESG academies designed to upskill all levels of staff, from front-line relationship managers to senior executives. These academies focus on sector-specific ESG risks, the design of sustainable finance products, and ethical decision-making. Icelandic banks could adapt these models to build deeper institutional capacity (Accenture, 2022). Incentive structures are also evolving. Globally, many banks are linking executive bonuses or team KPIs to ESG performance. For example, HSBC includes carbon reduction metrics in performance reviews, while BNP Paribas tracks sustainable loan origination targets. Among Icelandic banks, such practices remain limited. Embedding ESG into formal evaluation and reward systems would signal strategic importance and reinforce accountability (Eccles & Serafeim, 2013). Complementing these incentive mechanisms, banks are also expanding the scope of internal oversight to include ESG considerations. One underexplored area is the intersection between ESG roles and internal audit. Banks increasingly involve auditors in assessing the robustness of ESG reporting systems and the credibility of sustainability data. Integrating ESG audits into broader risk assurance frameworks ensures consistency and helps prevent greenwashing. Icelandic banks could enhance their ESG credibility by engaging internal audit functions early in sustainability initiatives (UNEP FI, 2019).

The internationalization of regulatory frameworks is another factor reshaping the roles of ESG. With the expansion of the EU Taxonomy and the CSRD, sustainability work is no longer voluntary or reputational, it is a legal obligation. This creates a need for legal literacy among ESG professionals and closer collaboration with legal and compliance departments (Jerónimo et al., 2020). Organizational culture continues to shape role effectiveness. In high-trust environments, sustainability champions can act autonomously, test innovations, and share feedback openly. In more hierarchical or compliance-driven cultures, ESG staff often operate with limited discretion and must navigate multiple levels of approval. Interviewees emphasized the importance of psychological safety, leadership visibility, and open channels for feedback in sustaining motivation and initiative. Ultimately, the long-term evolution of ESG roles must incorporate the emotional and political aspects of sustainability work. As the field grows more visible, it may become more contested, subject to pushback from those who view ESG mandates as costs rather than value generators. Sustainability staff may require training in technical topics, change management, negotiation, and political navigation. Building coalitions, aligning with financial objectives, and storytelling remain critical skills for gaining buy-in and influencing at scale (Lozano & Garcia, 2020). Expanding ESG roles within banks requires more than assigning new tasks. It involves professionalizing the field, embedding sustainability into incentive structures, leveraging technology, aligning with regulations, and fostering a culture that values long-term thinking. When these elements come together, sustainability professionals can act as implementers and strategic enablers, catalyzing innovation, reducing risk, and advancing institutional purpose.

4.2 Concluding Remarks

The evolution of sustainability roles in banks is at a critical juncture. As external pressures intensify and internal expectations evolve, the success of sustainability strategies increasingly hinges on how roles are structured, supported, and integrated. This chapter has demonstrated that while Icelandic banks have made significant progress, challenges persist regarding resource constraints, fragmented responsibilities, limited career pathways, and inadequate training. To navigate this complexity, banks must adopt a dual approach: professionalize ESG roles through formal structures and qualifications while fostering the relational and cultural foundations that allow these roles to thrive. Embedding sustainability into job descriptions, leadership programs, and reward systems can strengthen institutional commitment. Equally important is cultivating a sense of shared purpose and psychological safety that empowers professionals to lead change from within.

Looking forward, the banks that will lead in sustainable finance will treat ESG not as a compliance burden, but as a lever for transformation. This requires recognizing that roles are not static; they evolve as the organization matures in its sustainability. Supporting this evolution will depend on continued investment in capacity building, knowledge exchange, and adaptive governance. Ultimately, redefining who does what in sustainability is not just about task allocation; it is about building an institutional mindset where sustainability is seen as core to business, not peripheral. The individuals undertaking this work deserve recognition, support, and strategic alignment. Only then can sustainability become truly embedded, credible, and effective. It involves professionalizing the field, embedding sustainability into incentive structures, leveraging technology, aligning with regulations, and fostering a culture that values long-term thinking. When these elements come together, sustainability professionals can also act as strategic enablers, catalyzing innovation, reducing risk, and advancing institutional purpose.

References

Accenture. (2022). *ESG training in financial services: Preparing the board and executives*.

Bruno, A., & Lagasio, V. (2021). Corporate governance and sustainability disclosure: Evidence from the European banking sector. *Sustainability, 13*(11), 6160. https://doi.org/10.3390/su13116160

Eccles, R. G., & Serafeim, G. (2013). The performance frontier: Innovating for a sustainable strategy. *Harvard Business Review, 91*(5), 50–60.

IcelandSIF. (n.d.). *Sustainable finance and investment tools: Reports and dashboards.*

Institute Project Management. (2022). ESG and project governance standards.

Ioannou, I., & Serafeim, G. (2019). Corporate Sustainability: A Strategy? SSRN Electronic Journal. https://doi.org/10.2139/ssrn.3312191

Jerónimo, H. M., Arrau, P. A., & Martinho, C. (2020). Enhancing sustainability through organizational culture: A multiple case study. *Journal of Cleaner Production, 275*, 122944. https://doi.org/10.1016/j.jclepro.2020.122944

Lozano, R., & Garcia, R. (2020). Achieving corporate sustainability through organizational learning. *Journal of Cleaner Production, 258*, 120613. https://doi.org/10.1016/j.jclepro.2020.120613

Sideri, A. (2021). Symbolic management and sustainability: The illusion of green governance. *Environmental Policy and Governance, 31*(3), 234–245. https://doi.org/10.1002/eet.1923

Silvius, G. (2021). Sustainability in project management: A literature review and impact analysis. *Procedia Computer Science, 181*, 137–144. https://doi.org/10.1016/j.procs.2021.01.123

Simard, M., & Aubry, M. (2024). Innovation in sustainability governance: Role of project managers. *Project Management Journal.*

Tan, Y., & Tsionas, M. G. (2022). Modelling Sustainability Efficiency in Banking. *International Journal of Finance & Economics, 27*(3), 3754–3772. https://doi.org/10.1002/ijfe.2349

UNEP FI. (2019). Principles for responsible banking: Guidance document.

Chapter 5
Regulatory Compliance, Pressures, and Complexity

5.1 Chapter Content

Regulation has become one of the most potent forces shaping how banks approach sustainability. In recent years, a cascade of EU directives has placed increasing pressure on financial institutions to disclose their environmental and social impacts, assess sustainability-related risks, and align with broader climate targets. The (CSRD), the Sustainable Finance Disclosure Regulation (SFDR), and the EU Taxonomy are chief among these regulations. Each of these frameworks has specific requirements, but their combined effect reshapes banks' internal architecture (European Commission, 2023). For many of the banks interviewed, introducing these regulations was a turning point. Once managed through voluntary reporting and stakeholder engagement, sustainability became a compliance issue subject to external audit and legal scrutiny. Previously discussed were values and commitments. "Now we discuss audit trails and deadlines," said one of the sustainability officers. This shift prompted banks to reassign staff, create new roles, and embed sustainability more deeply into risk, finance, and legal departments (Lozano & Garcia, 2020). While regulation brought new legitimacy to sustainability work, it also brought new burdens. Interviewees described long hours spent interpreting regulatory texts, preparing for mandatory disclosures, and coordinating with external consultants. The complexity of the frameworks, each with its timelines, metrics, and language, created significant administrative overhead. Smaller banks, in particular, reported feeling overwhelmed. "It's not that we don't want to comply," one interviewee said. "It's that we don't have the people, the systems, or the time." The problem of overlapping frameworks emerged as a consistent theme. For example, while the SFDR focuses on financial product disclosures, the CSRD targets company-wide sustainability reporting, and the EU Taxonomy adds a layer of technical criteria for sustainable economic activities. Banks often struggled to map these frameworks onto one another, resulting in duplicated efforts and inconsistent data

S. Gudmundsdottir, T. O. Sigurjonsson, *Sustainability in Banks*, SpringerBriefs in Business, https://doi.org/10.1007/978-3-032-05637-5_5

(Bruno & Lagasio, 2021). Several banks responded by establishing cross-functional task forces to manage regulatory compliance. These task forces brought together representatives from sustainability, risk, compliance, finance, and IT. Their task was to ensure alignment, identify gaps, and streamline the reporting process. While effective in some cases, these efforts depended heavily on informal relationships and the willingness of departments to collaborate.

Technology played a critical role in regulatory compliance. Banks with robust data infrastructure and ESG reporting systems found it easier to manage disclosures. Others relied on spreadsheets, manual data entry, and ad hoc tools. Interviewees repeatedly emphasized the need for better data governance and automation. One bank was developing a "compliance cockpit," a digital dashboard that consolidated key ESG metrics across departments, however, such tools remained rare (IcelandSIF, n.d.). Interestingly, while some interviewees described regulation as a burden, others saw it as a strategic lever. "It gives us a mandate," said one sustainability lead and then added "Now we have something to stand on when we request data, support, or access." This perspective highlights the dual role of regulation it both constrains and empowers. In several banks, EU regulations prompted executive boards to prioritize sustainability, allocate budgets, and assign formal responsibility as suggested by Eccles & Serafeim (2013). Still, regulation also created new risks. The pressure to comply led some banks to focus narrowly on reporting, at the expense of broader transformation. "We're so busy filling in templates that we don't have time to think," one specialist said. There was also concern about "compliance fatigue," the sense that staff were becoming disengaged or cynical due to the sheer volume of new requirements. This fatigue was particularly acute in banks with smaller teams and fewer resources as suggeted by Sideri (2021). A further challenge was interpretation. Despite the volume of guidance documents and workshops provided by EU institutions, many requirements remained open to interpretation. This ambiguity created uncertainty and variation in how banks approached compliance. Some hired external consultants, while others relied on peer benchmarking. "We talk to other banks constantly," one officer explained. "Everyone is trying to figure it out together." The evolving nature of regulation added another layer of complexity. Requirements shifted as directives were revised, taxonomies expanded, and new rules proposed. Banks found it challenging to keep up. One manager described regulation as a "moving target," requiring constant surveillance and adaptation. This instability can complicate strategic planning and create tension between short-term compliance and long-term sustainability vision (Tan & Tsionas, 2022). Despite these challenges, many interviewees acknowledged the positive impact of regulation. It brought consistency, accountability, and comparability. It pushed banks to develop internal systems, measure performance, and consider previously overlooked risks. In this sense, regulation catalyzed compliance and organizational learning (UNEP FI, 2019). While regulation provides an important framework, it is unlikely to deliver meaningful sustainability outcomes. Without sufficient resources, effective governance, and committed leadership, compliance efforts may risk becoming merely procedural or superficial. To move beyond this, banks might consider treating regulatory requirements as obligations and opportunities to embed sustainability more deeply. When aligned with internal processes, regulation can help clarify roles, support coordination, and encourage consistent progress.

Some banks approached regulation not as an endpoint but as a foundation for broader sustainability integration. They embedded sustainability into internal control systems, linked ESG disclosures to strategy, and developed cross-departmental structures to ensure coherence. These banks saw regulation not as an interruption, but as a step toward maturity, as suggested by Eccles and Serafeim (2013). Moreover, regulation increasingly requires banks to quantify and disclose climate-related risks in their portfolios. This prompts institutions to enhance their scenario analysis, carbon accounting, and impact assessments. As banks develop capacity in these areas, the quality of data and insight increases. However, this also requires investment in new tools, staff training, and alignment between departments such as risk, credit, and sustainability (Bruno & Lagasio, 2021). In some cases, regulation prompted strategic changes in product development. Banks began offering sustainability-linked loans, also known as green mortgages, not solely for competitive advantage, but also to align with upcoming taxonomies. One bank developed a new "taxonomy-aligned product roadmap" that utilizes regulatory definitions to guide innovation. While this required legal and operational work, it created coherence between market offerings and policy goals as suggested by Lozano and Garcia (2020). Another area affected by regulation is third-party management. As part of CSRD and other directives, banks must now ensure their suppliers and partners meet sustainability criteria. This expanded the role of procurement departments, which now work closely with ESG teams to vet vendors. It also created friction when sustainability expectations exceeded what suppliers could deliver. This change illustrates how regulation can extend beyond the institution, necessitating broader engagement within the ecosystem (Jerónimo et al., 2020).

Although Icelandic banks do not operate across multiple EU jurisdictions, regulatory complexity still emerged as a challenge. Managers noted that aligning with evolving EU sustainability directives often required interpreting broad frameworks through a national lens. One manager explained, "You'd think EU law would mean one standard, but each country adds its flavor." This created uncertainty around audit expectations and reporting protocols, even within a single-country context, complicating efforts to maintain consistency (Nasdaq, 2020). Beyond these technical challenges, regulation has also contributed to a broader cultural shift within banks. The formalization of sustainability reporting has introduced a new language and structure that compels internal dialogue. Managers who once viewed sustainability as peripheral must now report on targets, KPIs, and risk exposure. This shift creates learning opportunities but realizing them depends on strong leadership, targeted education, and a shared strategic vision (Accenture, 2022).

5.2 Concluding Remarks

As this chapter demonstrates, regulation has become a central pillar in shaping sustainability structures and behaviors within the banking sector. While it introduces new levels of complexity, cost, and operational demand, it also provides critical leverage for institutional transformation. The most effective banks are not those that merely comply, but those that seize regulatory mandates as opportunities to innovate, integrate, and lead. Embedding regulation into strategy, governance, and culture enables institutions to transition from reactive reporting to proactive sustainability management. This includes aligning ESG targets with strategic priorities, investing in digital tools for compliance, and fostering cross-functional teams equipped to navigate regulatory ambiguity. Importantly, education and internal communication are crucial in promoting a culture that not only understands the "what" of compliance but also the "why." As the regulatory environment evolves, banks must invest in structural and cultural agility. The institutions that thrive will be those that can adapt quickly, learn continuously, and integrate sustainability across all levels of their operations. Regulation is not a static destination but a dynamic force for long-term institutional learning and competitive advantage.

References

Accenture. (2022). *ESG training in financial services: Preparing the board and executives*.

Bruno, A., & Lagasio, V. (2021). Corporate governance and sustainability disclosure: Evidence from the European banking sector. *Sustainability, 13*(11), 6160. https://doi.org/10.3390/su13116160

Eccles, R. G., & Serafeim, G. (2013). The performance frontier: Innovating for a sustainable strategy. *Harvard Business Review, 91*(5), 50–60.

European Commission. (2023). EU sustainable finance framework: Regulations and directives overview. https://finance.ec.europa.eu

IcelandSIF. (n.d.). *Sustainable finance and investment tools: Reports and dashboards*.

Jerónimo, H. M., Arrau, P. A., & Martinho, C. (2020). Enhancing sustainability through organizational culture: A multiple case study. *Journal of Cleaner Production, 275*, 122944. https://doi.org/10.1016/j.jclepro.2020.122944

Lozano, R., & Garcia, R. (2020). Achieving corporate sustainability through organizational learning. *Journal of Cleaner Production, 258*, 120613. https://doi.org/10.1016/j.jclepro.2020.120613

Nasdaq. (2020). *ESG reporting guide for European companies*.

Sideri, A. (2021). Symbolic management and sustainability: The illusion of green governance. *Environmental Policy and Governance, 31*(3), 234–245. https://doi.org/10.1002/eet.1923

Tan, Q., & Tsionas, M. (2022). Innovation governance and ESG: Strategic alignment in banking. *Journal of Banking & Finance, 142*, 106491.

UNEP FI. (2019). Principles for responsible banking: Guidance document.

Chapter 6
Organizational Culture, Mindsets, and the Sustainability Narrative

6.1 Chapter Content

Organizational culture is pivotal in how sustainability is interpreted, implemented, and ultimately embedded in banking institutions. Unlike formal structures or reporting lines, culture resides in shared norms, values, behaviors, and beliefs that shape how individuals understand and react to sustainability initiatives (Schein, 2004). Culture manifests through everyday language, behavior, decision-making processes, and the allocation of attention and resources. Interviewees consistently described culture as the "invisible force" shaping outcomes. At one bank, a sustainability lead remarked, "You can incorporate sustainability into the strategy, the organizational chart, and the KPIs. However, if the mindset hasn't changed, nothing changes". This perspective aligns with institutional work theory, emphasizing that lasting change is impossible without cultural alignment (Jerónimo et al., 2020). Language emerged as one of the most precise indicators of cultural orientation. The use of financial metaphors, such as "return on sustainability," "carbon as risk," or "green premiums," made sustainability more comprehensible to executives, thereby increasing its internal legitimacy (Bruno & Lagasio, 2021). However, this also introduced limitations. When sustainability is viewed only through a financial lens, its broader ethical and societal dimensions risk being overlooked.

The cultural valuation of sustainability professionals varied widely. In some banks, ESG teams were seen as strategic partners, in others, they were marginalized or excluded from core decision-making processes. Such disparities reflect broader cultural norms around expertise and power. When sustainability is viewed as "non-core," it becomes challenging to establish cross-functional partnerships or access sufficient resources (Lozano & Garcia, 2020). Cultural archetypes observed across the four case banks revealed how historical identity influenced sustainability narratives. For instance, one bank leveraged its tradition of community engagement as a cultural anchor, integrating sustainability as a natural extension of its legacy.

S. Gudmundsdottir, T. O. Sigurjonsson, *Sustainability in Banks*, SpringerBriefs in Business, https://doi.org/10.1007/978-3-032-05637-5_6

Another, with a history of risk aversion, adopted a more cautious, compliance-driven approach. These findings align with the literature, which suggests that pre-existing cultural identities shape the strategic framing of sustainability (Eccles & Serafeim, 2013). Informal networks and cultural brokers played a vital role in promoting sustainability. These individuals, often without formal authority, acted as connectors across departments. Their influence was rooted in trust, relational capital, and a nuanced understanding of organizational dynamics. Empowering such actors can accelerated internal diffusion of sustainability practices as suggested by Simard & Aubry (2024). Resistance to sustainability was frequently cultural rather than technical. While most banks possessed the tools and knowledge to initiate implementation, longstanding norms surrounding profitability, hierarchy, and autonomy hindered progress. For example, commercial departments were wary of sustainability-linked lending, fearing it might strain client relationships. This type of resistance underscores how deeply entrenched mental models can override institutional ambitions (Sideri, 2021). Top-down leadership and grassroots activism both played essential roles in shifting the culture. Executive participation in sustainability initiatives sent powerful signals about organizational priorities. At the same time, employee-driven green teams and innovation projects helped foster ownership and experimentation. Successful banks are known to have harnessed both forces to reinforce alignment and sustain momentum (UNEP FI, 2019). Storytelling emerged as a strategic tool. Stories about renewable energy financing, customer demands for ESG compliance, or successful pilot programs helped bridge the gap between abstract goals and daily work. Storytelling is well-established as a cultural mechanism that creates meaning, fosters identity, and facilitates sense-making during times of change (Schein, 2004).

Debates over measurement reflected cultural tensions. Some departments prioritized KPIs and dashboards, while others questioned the adequacy of quantitative metrics. "You can measure carbon, but can you measure dignity?" one interviewee asked. This reflects a broader struggle between managerialism and value-based approaches to sustainability (Tan & Tsionas, 2022). Generational dynamics also influenced culture. Younger staff were described as more values-driven and vocal in their advocacy for climate action. Nevertheless, their enthusiasm often faded without career development pathways or strategic influence. Banks that created structured roles for early-career staff in ESG initiatives were more successful in maintaining momentum and engagement. Sustainability culture was most potent in banks where values, behaviors, and symbols were aligned. This included leadership signaling, consistent communication, embedded ESG competencies, and recognition for sustainability efforts. These banks treated culture as not an intangible side effect but a core strategic asset as suggested by Lozano & Garcia (2020). However, cultivating such a culture was not without obstacles. Resistance emerged not only from individual skepticism but also from deeper systemic misalignments. Performance metrics, organizational silos, and legacy business models often reinforced short-term thinking. Many banks lacked formal mechanisms to reward sustainability efforts, further entrenching the perception that ESG work was non-essential. Strategies to overcome resistance included change management, training, internal communications, and leadership modeling. Banks that mapped cultural friction points and co-created solutions with employees reported greater success. Importantly, resistance was reframed not as failure, but as an indicator of where alignment and engagement were most needed, as noted by Jerónimo et al. (2020). Organizational learning structures played a critical role in bridging these gaps. Forums, ESG communities of practice, and sustainability incubators were particularly effective in fostering engagement. These spaces offered psychological safety, peer support, and opportunities to iterate solutions. By investing in such systems, banks enabled their cultures to evolve dynamically with strategic goals as suggested by Silvius (2021).

An emerging area of focus in cultural transformation involves the shift from compliance-based thinking to purpose-driven engagement. Many banks interviewed in the study acknowledged that early sustainability efforts were primarily motivated by external pressures, regulatory demands, investor expectations, or reputational concerns. However, transitioning to a mature sustainability culture requires a more intrinsic motivation anchored in the bank's mission, values, and commitment to social good. As such, banks are increasingly using visioning workshops, internal storytelling campaigns, and purpose audits to reconnect teams with a broader sense of why sustainability matters (Lozano & Garcia, 2020). Cultural shifts also depend on how power and authority are exercised in sustainability contexts. Banks' sustainability decisions were sometimes centralized in compliance or risk units, reinforcing a hierarchical control model. While efficient in ensuring minimum standards, this approach often disempowered operational teams and reduced innovation. In contrast, banks that distributed responsibility, allowing product managers, analysts, and customer-facing staff to co-create sustainability practices, fostered deeper engagement and more tailored solutions. These insights suggest a need to recalibrate governance models to reflect participatory principles (Silvius, 2021). Furthermore, research suggests that microcultures within large organizations can have a significant impact on sustainability outcomes. A risk team may be conservative and metrics-driven, while the communications department embraces storytelling and brand alignment. Identifying and bridging these subcultures is crucial. Some banks have adopted rotating ESG roles or cross-departmental immersion programs, enabling staff to experience different cultural perspectives and foster a shared understanding.

One underexplored aspect of culture is the influence of emotion and identity on sustainability behaviors. Employees who see sustainability as part of their professional identity are more likely to act as champions and resist cultural backsliding. Banks can tap into this by recognizing emotional labor, providing spaces for value alignment, and celebrating personal sustainability journeys. This approach also fosters resilience, a crucial trait in navigating complex and uncertain ESG challenges. The symbolic dimension of culture also merits attention. From the design of workspaces to the language of annual reports, symbols communicate what matters. One bank redesigned its headquarters to incorporate sustainability exhibits, green spaces, and energy dashboards visible in public areas. Another adopted a "sustainability signature," a short statement in every internal memo and board document. Such symbols help embed sustainability in the institutional fabric and remind staff of their shared mission (Simard & Aubry, 2024). Banks are also experimenting with rituals and ceremonies that reinforce cultural norms. Sustainability awards, internal challenges, and milestone celebrations create moments of recognition and renewal. These practices, while informal, signal commitment and reinforce desired behaviors. Organizational anthropology emphasizes the significance of such rituals in maintaining cultural continuity and facilitating change (Schein, 2004).

Finally, the role of external actors in shaping internal culture is increasingly evident. Stakeholders, including NGOs, regulators, investors, and customers, act as cultural influencers. Their expectations and feedback, as expressed through audits, media scrutiny, or shareholder resolutions, shape how the bank understands and acts upon sustainability. Strategic engagement with these actors, both in PR and in co-design and learning, enhances cultural responsiveness and authenticity (UNEP FI, 2019). These expanded insights show that building a sustainability-oriented culture is not a static goal but a dynamic practice. It involves rewiring habits, assumptions, and symbols across all levels of the organization. It requires humility, creativity, and persistence. Most importantly, it demands that banks recognize culture not as a passive backdrop, but as an active, evolving force shaping the future of sustainable finance.

6.2 Concluding Remarks

Culture is not merely an enabler of sustainability; it is the soil in which sustainability flourishes or withers. As this chapter has shown, organizational culture permeates every level of bank operations, shaping how sustainability is perceived, prioritized, and practiced. From narratives and language to decision-making processes and informal networks, culture plays a defining role in aligning institutions with the long-term vision of sustainability. Banks that succeed in embedding sustainability into their DNA do not rely solely on regulations, reporting structures, or compliance mechanisms. They invest in cultural transformation through leadership engagement, inclusive dialogue, celebrating successes, and empowering grassroots change agents. Culture is the connective tissue that binds strategy to practice and aspiration to execution. However, cultural change is complex, uneven, and sometimes uncomfortable. Resistance is a natural part of this journey. The challenge for banks is to recognize resistance not as an obstacle to overcome, but as a signal to listen more closely, engage more deeply, and lead with empathy. In doing so, banks can turn moments of tension into opportunities for growth and renewal. The chapter has emphasized that fostering a sustainability-oriented culture is a dynamic, iterative process. It cannot be reduced to a checklist or outsourced to a single team. It must be lived, reinforced, and reflected in the daily rhythms of organizational life, from how meetings are run to how success is defined. Banks can only fully unlock their potential to act as catalysts for a more sustainable economy through this cultural realignment. In conclusion, culture is not solely the product of top-down management, but rather evolves through everyday practices, shared values, and collective engagement. Fostering a long-term, purpose-oriented mindset grounded in inclusion, integrity, and innovation can support a more meaningful integration of sustainability goals. In doing so, banks position themselves to meet regulatory and stakeholder expectations and contribute to the broader development of sustainable finance.

References

Bruno, A., & Lagasio, V. (2021). Corporate governance and sustainability disclosure: Evidence from the European banking sector. *Sustainability, 13*(11), 6160. https://doi.org/10.3390/su13116160

Eccles, R. G., & Serafeim, G. (2013). The performance frontier: Innovating for a sustainable strategy. *Harvard Business Review, 91*(5), 50–60.

Jerónimo, H. M., Arrau, P. A., & Martinho, C. (2020). Enhancing sustainability through organizational culture: A multiple case study. *Journal of Cleaner Production, 275*, 122944. https://doi.org/10.1016/j.jclepro.2020.122944

Lozano, R., & Garcia, R. (2020). Achieving corporate sustainability through organizational learning. *Journal of Cleaner Production, 258*, 120613. https://doi.org/10.1016/j.jclepro.2020.120613

Schein, E. H. (2004). *Organizatioal culture and leaderhip* (3rd ed.). Josey-Bass.

Sideri, A. (2021). Symbolic management and sustainability: The illusion of green governance. *Environmental Policy and Governance, 31*(3), 234–245. https://doi.org/10.1002/eet.1923

Silvius, G. (2021). Sustainability in project management: A literature review and impact analysis. *Procedia Computer Science, 181*, 137–144. https://doi.org/10.1016/j.procs.2021.01.123

Simard, M., & Aubry, M. (2024). Innovation in sustainability governance: Role of project managers. *Project Management Journal.*

Tan, Q., & Tsionas, M. (2022). Innovation governance and ESG: Strategic alignment in banking. *Journal of Banking & Finance, 142*, 106491.

UNEP FI. (2019). Principles for responsible banking: Guidance document.

Chapter 7
Project Management and Strategic Implementation

7.1 Chapter Content

Project management has emerged as a critical tool for integrating sustainability into bank operations. It is the structured yet flexible arena where strategy meets execution, where high-level sustainability commitments are translated into specific actions, timelines, and outcomes. As banks grapple with complex regulatory expectations, shifting stakeholder demands, and internal cultural transitions, the Project Management Office (PMO) and related project governance structures are increasingly being called upon to facilitate and lead the sustainability transformation (Morris, 2020). The PMO (or an equivalent project and transformation unit) played varied but influential roles in structuring sustainability work in the four case banks examined for this study. In Bank A, the PMO acted as a central gatekeeper, coordinating and embedding all strategic sustainability initiatives into the bank's annual planning cycle. In Bank B, the PMO maintained a looser oversight role, providing methodologies and support while leaving execution to functional departments. Bank C, characterized by a decentralized structure, had multiple project managers embedded across units but lacked a unified strategy for sustainability projects. Bank D was creating a Sustainability PMO specifically to oversee green finance, emissions reduction efforts, and ESG compliance.

Positioning sustainability projects within PMO portfolios affects visibility, accountability, and resource allocation. When sustainability is treated like any other strategic priority with milestones, owners, and evaluation metrics, it is more likely to receive consistent attention and cross-departmental engagement (Silvius, 2021). In contrast, when sustainability projects are placed on the periphery or lack executive sponsorship, they risk being overshadowed by traditional business initiatives. One of the strengths of the project management approach lies in its ability to bridge silos. Sustainability requires coordination between departments that may not normally interact, such as legal and marketing, HR and operations, IT, and risk. Projects

S. Gudmundsdottir, T. O. Sigurjonsson, *Sustainability in Banks*, SpringerBriefs in Business, https://doi.org/10.1007/978-3-032-05637-5_7

bring these units together under shared goals, timelines, and deliverables. This cross-pollination not only accelerates learning but also enhances alignment. Interviewees repeatedly emphasized the importance of cross-functional task forces and interdepartmental steering committees in ensuring that sustainability efforts were not fragmented or redundant.

Projects also serve as catalysts for cultural change. They provide concrete opportunities for employees to experiment with new practices, metrics, and mindsets. For example, one bank launched a pilot project that integrates ESG risk assessments into its credit decisions. While initially limited to a small product line, the project allowed credit officers, sustainability experts, and data analysts to co-create new workflows, test assumptions, and iterate. The pilot's success built internal confidence and was later scaled across the bank. Interviewees highlighted the importance of having clear project charters, strong executive sponsors, and dedicated resources. Several noted that part-time personnel, who struggled to balance competing priorities, often had underfunded or understaffed sustainability projects. Where project teams were fully resourced, given decision-making authority, and supported by senior leaders, sustainability outcomes improved significantly as suggested by Tan and Tsionas (2022).

A recurring theme was the strategic use of champions, individuals embedded in business units who serve as liaisons between project teams and operational staff. These champions play a critical role in communication, training, and troubleshooting. Their credibility within the unit often determines whether a sustainability initiative is embraced or resisted. Banks that invested in developing champions (through training, recognition, and career incentives) reported higher project uptake and smoother implementation. In addition to traditional project planning tools, several banks began using sustainability-specific templates, including ESG impact assessments, climate scenario planning modules, and green procurement checklists. These tools helped standardize approaches while reinforcing the message that sustainability was a core strategic concern, as suggested by Bruno and Lagasio (2021). Importantly, projects were often the first visible manifestation of a bank's sustainability strategy. While strategies may be outlined in glossy reports, projects demonstrate action. As one manager said, "Our strategy lives and dies by our projects. That's how people judge whether we're serious." The strategic alignment of sustainability projects with long-term planning processes remains an area of improvement. Interviewees noted that while short-term projects were abundant, few banks had clear roadmaps connecting these efforts to long-term goals, such as five- or ten-year objectives. The absence of a programmatic approach led to project fatigue and limited institutional learning. Banks that began clustering sustainability projects into broader programs such as "Net Zero Transformation" or "Green Lending Innovation" were better able to track progress and build momentum. The need for effective coordination tools became increasingly apparent as these programs gained structure. The role of digital tools and project management systems cannot be overstated. Banks with centralized platforms for tracking sustainability projects, KPIs, and interdependencies found it easier to scale initiatives and share knowledge. These systems also provided transparency for boards, auditors, and external stakeholders.

Advanced banks are increasingly applying project portfolio management (PPM) principles to their sustainability agendas. This involves managing individual sustainability projects, evaluating their contribution to overall objectives, managing risks, and optimizing resource utilization. Some banks have introduced sustainability dashboards within their enterprise project management platforms, enabling executives to view performance across ESG-related initiatives. These tools provide clarity and support prioritization, especially in constrained resources. Additionally, banks are experimenting with co-creation models, in which external partners, such as fintech startups, regulators, or NGOs, are integrated into sustainability projects. These partnerships often inject fresh perspectives and innovation, but they also require new governance frameworks to manage intellectual property, data sharing, and reputational risk. Several interviewees described pilot collaborations that began as limited experiments but grew into strategic alliances.

Leadership and change management practices also play a significant role in determining the success of sustainability project portfolios. Leaders who communicate a clear vision, provide sustained support, and encourage learning from failure are more likely to see meaningful results. In contrast, projects suffer when treated as checkboxes or short-term campaigns. Building on this foundation, some banks are beginning to embed sustainability into their core systems deeply. In the final phase of project maturity, some banks have embedded sustainability into their enterprise architecture and digital systems. This includes automating ESG data flows, integrating carbon accounting into product development systems, and using AI-driven insights to support sustainable investment decisions. These advanced practices suggest that the future of project-based sustainability will be more strategic and technologically enabled. As banks become more sophisticated, they also document and share their project methodologies through knowledge management systems, internal toolkits, and training programs. These efforts institutionalize learning and help scale successful practices across teams and geographies. Ultimately, project management offers banks a unique and powerful tool to implement sustainability in an actionable, measurable way, aligned with their broader business strategy. Banks can transform isolated initiatives into system-wide change by investing in mature project practices.

7.2 Concluding Remarks

This chapter has shown that project management is a vital engine for advancing sustainability within banks. Far beyond isolated tasks, sustainability projects provide a structured space where strategic vision is translated into action. The Project Management Office (PMO), cross-functional teams, and internal champions serve as key vehicles for bridging silos, mobilizing resources, and building internal alignment. When supported by transparent governance, dedicated leadership, and appropriate tools, projects can accelerate both organizational learning and cultural transformation. A critical insight emerging from the case studies is that project-based approaches are most effective when linked to broader institutional goals. Banks that cluster sustainability projects into coherent programs such as "Net Zero Transformation" or "Green Lending Innovation" can better maintain momentum, track progress, and reduce project fatigue. Digital systems and centralized dashboards enhance transparency, scalability, and cross-departmental coordination. Leadership and change management practices significantly shape project outcomes. Leaders who provide a clear mandate, encourage experimentation, and invest in internal capacity help create an environment where sustainability is not just a compliance exercise but a strategic priority. As banks move toward more mature integration stages, sustainability is embedded into enterprise systems, decision-making processes, and digital architectures.

Looking ahead, the role of project management in sustainable finance will only grow in importance. It offers a flexible yet disciplined framework for navigating complexity, aligning internal efforts, and responding to evolving regulatory and stakeholder demands. Banks can move from ad hoc initiatives to systemic, strategic transformation by investing in robust project governance and portfolio management capabilities.

References

Bruno, L., & Lagasio, V. (2021). ESG and bank performance: A European perspective. *Sustainability, 13*(23), 13011.

Morris, P. W. G. (2020). *Reconstructing project management*. Wiley.

Silvius, G. (2021). Sustainability in project management: A literature review and impact analysis. *Procedia Computer Science, 181*, 703–710.

Tan, K. H., & Tsionas, M. (2022). Managing sustainability projects in financial institutions. *International Journal of Project Management, 40*(2), 112–127.

Chapter 8
From Periphery to Core: Comparative Insights and Integrated Pathways for Sustainability in Banking

Before turning to the individual case banks, it is helpful to briefly outline the rationale for this comparative approach. Each case was chosen to reflect a distinct organizational pathway shaped by a shared regulatory environment but differing leadership priorities, cultural orientation, and structural choices. The goal here is not to prescribe a single model of sustainability integration, but to offer insight into how diverse institutions are navigating the transition. This analysis also anticipates the framework elaborated in Chap. 9, titled, Embedding Sustainability: A Framework for Organizational Transformation in Banking, which synthesizes six interdependent pillars: strategic alignment, distributed ownership, data infrastructure, cultural coherence, capacity building, and project-based implementation. These dimensions serve as reference points throughout the case analysis, providing a conceptual thread that runs through both chapters. In doing so, this chapter highlights the enabling conditions and persistent challenges that shape the institutionalization of ESG practices in Icelandic banking.

8.1 Bank A: Centralized Strategy with Executive Sponsorship

Bank A exemplifies the institutional logic of strategy-led integration, where sustainability gains organizational legitimacy through proximity to power. Initially housed in Communications, ESG functions were repositioned under the Strategy Office following the appointment of a CEO with international sustainability experience. This structural shift marked a turning point, aligning with Lozano's (2015) argument that executive sponsorship is crucial for institutionalizing sustainability. A cross-functional ESG steering group, chaired by the CEO, brought together leaders from risk, legal, HR, operations, and compliance, enabling vertical and horizontal integration. ESG indicators were integrated into KPIs, budgets, and product

S. Gudmundsdottir, T. O. Sigurjonsson, *Sustainability in Banks*, SpringerBriefs in Business, https://doi.org/10.1007/978-3-032-05637-5_8

development processes. The PMO was instructed to prioritize sustainability-linked initiatives, and annual planning cycles incorporated ESG criteria. Bank A also aligned financial incentives with sustainability by introducing dual KPIs for volume and ESG impact, which required negotiation across departments but reinforced internal consistency. Staff were further engaged through storytelling and symbolic actions, such as naming internal initiatives after SDGs. One sustainability lead remarked, "Our projects were where silos broke down." Projects served as testing grounds for innovation. A pilot sustainable mortgage product linked interest rates to energy efficiency, requiring collaboration across IT, risk, marketing, and compliance. These initiatives were supported by centralized dashboards that enabled real-time tracking of ESG metrics across departments, improving accountability and learning.

8.2 Bank B: Risk-Driven Realignment and Tactical Adaptation

Bank B took a different path, framing sustainability as a compliance and risk management issue. ESG functions were integrated into risk and compliance, creating formal oversight mechanisms, but this integration narrowed the scope of ESG to reporting and controls. This reflected a logic of risk mitigation (Thornton & Ocasio, 1999). Instead of a dedicated ESG team, responsibilities were distributed across existing roles. This was intended to foster shared ownership, but it often led to fragmentation. One officer noted, "Everyone has a piece of the puzzle, but no one sees the whole picture." Credit risk and green lending projects were launched, but these remained tactical. Still, Bank B made strides in building cultural engagement. A monthly "green stories" newsletter highlighted staff contributions to ESG efforts, and symbolic actions such as celebrating ESG milestones helped legitimize the work. ESG data systems enabled simulations to evaluate the environmental impacts of lending, leading to the development of innovative products. Agile methods were applied in project teams, enabling faster feedback and cross-departmental collaboration. Despite its compliance-first framing, Bank B's initiatives showed how even risk-centric models can evolve toward strategic alignment when supported by data tools, storytelling, and distributed innovation.

8.3 Bank C: Decentralized Experimentation and Cultural Resistance

Bank C demonstrated a more fragmented approach. Without a central ESG structure, sustainability initiatives emerged independently within departments. While this encouraged local innovation, it led to misalignment and inconsistent accountability. Interviewees described a culture marked by hierarchy and conservatism. Even where champions existed, their efforts were isolated due to a lack of senior support. This reflects Christensen et al.'s (2013) caution against aspirational talk unsupported by structural mechanisms. Data systems were underdeveloped, with ESG information gathered manually. "Every quarter it's a scramble," one manager admitted. Moreover, conflicting priorities were a persistent challenge: "We're expected to meet loan goals and reduce emissions, but no one tells us what takes priority." Still, recent attempts to benchmark peer practices and standardize reporting indicate some institutional learning. Bank C's case highlights the importance of cultural coherence and strategic clarity to sustain decentralized efforts.

8.4 Bank D: Emerging Integration Through Governance Innovation

Bank D represents a newer, more deliberate approach. Responding to regulatory and investor pressures, the bank formed a board-level ESG committee and a sustainability department within the strategy office. This hybrid model centralized coordination while distributing operational responsibility. The sustainability team functioned as a knowledge hub, running training, communications, and engagement activities. ESG focal points in each department acted as liaisons, bridging strategy and operations. Bank D also experimented with agile projects, such as a 12-week "green sprint" to develop a carbon-conscious credit product, demonstrating rapid innovation and team learning. Beyond innovation labs, Bank D also invested in embedding ESG into talent pathways. Sustainability competencies were included in performance reviews, and ESG aptitude was a consideration in leadership succession planning. This institutionalized approach helped move sustainability from a niche concern to a shared organizational responsibility. One HR executive noted, "We no longer consider ESG optional. It's embedded in how we identify and prepare our future leaders." These efforts were supported by cross-functional learning forums and internal ESG certification programs, reinforcing Bank D's role as a learning organization. Real-time ESG dashboards enhance transparency and collaboration. Sustainability was included in talent management and succession planning, fostering long-term capacity. These elements reflect the six-pillar framework for ESG integration: strategic alignment, distributed ownership, data infrastructure, cultural coherence, capacity building, and project-based implementation. Bank D treated regulation not as a ceiling but as a foundation for broader engagement. By linking internal and external expectations, the bank advanced a co-creation logic aligned with adaptive governance (Thornton & Ocasio, 1999).

8.5 Concluding Remarks

This comparative analysis illustrates the multifaceted nature of sustainability integration. While all four banks operated under similar regulatory frameworks, their internal pathways diverged sharply, shaped by leadership, structure, culture, and institutional logic. Banks A and D demonstrated how aligned structures, clear mandates, and cultural reinforcement can effectively embed ESG across their operations. Their use of cross-functional teams, real-time data, and agile projects enabled learning and innovation. Bank B's risk-centric model evolved through storytelling and project agility, while Bank C's decentralization revealed the limits of innovation without coordination or cultural support. Integrating insights from a holistic framework reveals that effective ESG implementation is not about copying best practices, but rather about aligning key elements: strategy, ownership, data, culture, capacity, and projects. These components are deeply interdependent. When coordinated, they create self-reinforcing dynamics that strengthen sustainability over time. Institutionalization is not linear. Conflicts between legacy and emerging logics persist. Nevertheless, banks that invest in alignment and learning are more likely to turn external pressure into strategic foresight. Sustainability becomes a compliance requirement and a lens through which to define purpose, build resilience, and generate long-term value.

Looking ahead, banks aiming to strengthen their ESG integration can benefit from assessing maturity across the six pillars identified here. A diagnostic approach that examines alignment, ownership, culture, capacity, data systems, and project governance can identify gaps and inform investment decisions. Crucially, these dimensions should not be treated in isolation. Success lies in their interaction when data informs strategy, when projects build culture, and when leadership empowers distributed ownership. By designing systems that support this interplay, banks can create resilient structures capable of adapting to the evolving sustainability landscape.

References

Christensen, L. T., Morsing, M., & Thyssen, O. (2013). CSR as aspirational talk. *Organization, 20*(3), 372–393. https://doi.org/10.1177/1350508413478310

Lozano, R. (2015). A holistic perspective on corporate sustainability drivers. *Corporate Social Responsibility and Environmental Management, 22*(1), 32–44. https://doi.org/10.1002/csr.1325

Thornton, P. H., & Ocasio, W. (1999). Institutional logics and the historical contingency of power in organizations: Executive succession in the higher education publishing industry, 1958–1990. *American Journal of Sociology, 105*(3), 801–843. https://doi.org/10.1086/210361

Chapter 9
Embedding Sustainability: A Framework for Organizational Transformation in Banking

9.1 Chapter Content

Building on previous chapters, the flowing content synthesizes the above themes into a practical and conceptual framework for institutionalizing sustainability in banking. The aim is not to offer a prescriptive checklist, but to identify core building blocks that support integration in diverse organizational contexts. Each pillar is grounded in empirical insights from Icelandic banks and reflects broader trends in sustainable finance. It comprises six interdependent and mutually reinforcing elements that support the institutionalization of sustainability. These components are: (1) strategic alignment and executive mandate, (2) distributed ownership with central coordination, (3) integrated data systems and digital infrastructure, (4) cultural alignment and narrative coherence, (5) capacity building and incentive alignment, and (6) project-based implementation with feedback loops.

Each element is explored in detail, drawing on real-world examples from four Icelandic banks at different stages of their sustainability journeys. The chapter highlights how leadership visibility and strategic intent anchor ESG efforts, while distributed structures enhance relevance and continuity across departments. It examines how digital tools and data architecture support both compliance and innovation, and how cultural narratives influence the level of internal engagement. Furthermore, it demonstrates how investments in training, performance systems, and symbolic incentives foster the human capital necessary to drive sustainability forward. Ultimately, it highlights the significance of cross-functional projects and iterative learning in translating sustainability goals into practical applications.

Through this multi-dimensional framework, the chapter offers practical guidance to banks seeking to move beyond isolated ESG initiatives and toward system-wide integration. It emphasizes that successful ESG transformation requires more than structural change, it demands a shift in how organizations think, learn, and operate concerning sustainability. This framework, as can be seen in Fig. 9.1, thus serves as

S. Gudmundsdottir, T. O. Sigurjonsson, *Sustainability in Banks*, SpringerBriefs in Business, https://doi.org/10.1007/978-3-032-05637-5_9

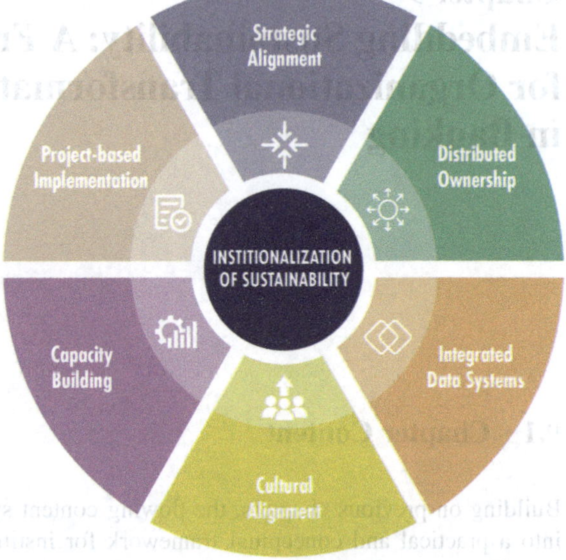

Fig. 9.1 Framework for institutionalization of sustainability

both a diagnostic tool and a roadmap for action, offering a lens through which banks can assess their internal readiness for long-term sustainability transformation.

Strategic Alignment and Executive Mandate

This section emphasizes the importance of aligning sustainability efforts closely with the bank's core strategic objectives. Strategic alignment refers to integrating sustainability into the bank's core mission, strategic priorities, and performance targets. In leading banks, ESG objectives are embedded in strategic documents, executive KPIs, and financial planning processes. Alignment ensures sustainability is not a parallel agenda, but a lens through which core activities are assessed and resourced. Strategic alignment begins with a top leadership commitment, symbolic endorsement, and the practical integration of ESG priorities into decision-making processes, performance metrics, and resource allocation. In the cases analyzed, banks that successfully advanced their sustainability agendas treated ESG as integral to value creation, not a peripheral obligation. Moreover, strategic alignment is reinforced when sustainability responsibilities are reflected in the formal mandates of executive teams and board governance structures. Some banks further linked ESG targets to executive compensation and incorporated sustainability indicators into business performance dashboards. This ensured that sustainability remained visible and relevant across planning horizons.

At the same time, alignment is not a one-off declaration, it requires continuous iteration. As external expectations evolve, so must the internal articulation of sustainability goals. Leadership must periodically reframe the strategic narrative to ensure it resonates with external stakeholders and internal staff. In this sense, strategic alignment becomes an ongoing act of translation and sense-making, rather than a fixed statement of intent. Strategic alignment begins with executive sponsorship and board-level mandates. In Bank A, placing sustainability within the CEO's office enabled ESG considerations to shape annual planning and performance evaluation, illustrating how structural positioning influences decision-making (Eccles et al., 2014). Without visible executive support, sustainability efforts often lack the legitimacy to scale. Leadership must communicate a clear vision, align ESG goals with business objectives, and institutionalize this alignment through planning cycles and incentive systems (Lozano, 2015).

In Bank A, the executive mandate for sustainability was accompanied by the development of mid-term transformation roadmaps, which linked ESG targets with digitalization and customer experience goals. These roadmaps were embedded into planning processes through cascading OKRs (Objectives and Key Results), ensuring that even team-level KPIs reflected sustainability ambitions. Interviewees emphasized that the increased visibility of executive involvement led to greater accountability at all levels. One senior officer remarked, "Once the CEO linked our ESG goals to our loan portfolio growth targets, it was no longer an option. It became a strategic lever." This transition reflects the shift from sustainability as a policy narrative to an internal driver of performance.

Distributed Ownership with Central Coordination

Distributed ownership is fundamental for embedding sustainability across all levels of the organization. Distributed ownership moves sustainability responsibility beyond a central unit. While dedicated ESG teams coordinate, true institutionalization depends on operational units taking ownership. Banks in the study achieved this through dual-reporting structures, ESG focal points in departments, and cross-functional steering groups. This approach creates accountability and contextual relevance, requiring ongoing coordination to prevent fragmentation.

Rather than confining ESG to a dedicated unit, banks increasingly recognize that effective implementation depends on the engagement of multiple departments and teams. However, without central coordination, distributed ownership risks become fragmented, leading to inconsistent practices, diluted accountability, and missed opportunities for integration (Lafioune et al., 2023).

Successful models combine transparent central governance with local adaptation. A central ESG unit or coordinator typically developed the strategy in the banks studied, provided guidance and resources, and monitored overall progress. At the same time, operational units were given the autonomy to tailor sustainability initiatives to their functions and client relationships. This dual approach ensured that ESG aligned with institutional goals and meaningful to front-line teams (Carlsson et al., 2023). Several institutions formalized this model by creating cross-functional

ESG steering committees or sustainability councils. These bodies included representatives from key departments, risk, compliance, operations, HR, and IT and provided a platform for coordination and mutual learning. Additionally, many banks relied on informal networks of ESG champions who served as translators and brokers between strategy and practice (Tangi et al., 2020). These champions often played a crucial role in translating top-down objectives into actionable initiatives. Clear delineation of roles and responsibilities was essential. Banks with defined ESG mandates in job descriptions, performance evaluations, and departmental key performance indicators (KPIs) experienced greater internal engagement. This also helped to move sustainability beyond the ESG team, signaling that it was a shared responsibility across the organization (Lafioune et al., 2023). Trust, relational capacity, and communication infrastructure were equally important. Institutions with pre-existing cultures of cross-functional collaboration adapted more quickly to distributed ESG governance. Central teams focused on enabling and supporting rather than controlling local efforts tended to build more substantial buy-in and alignment. One interviewee said, "We act as a resource, not a watchdog."

Integrated Data Systems and Digital Infrastructure

Data infrastructure supports credibility, comparability, and compliance. Banks with mature ESG systems have integrated sustainability data into risk, credit, and finance dashboards. Technology played a crucial role in enabling transparency and reducing manual effort. Conversely, weak data systems led to duplication and undermined decision-making. The ability to measure, manage, and monitor sustainability performance depends increasingly on robust data systems and digital infrastructure. Banks that treat data as a strategic asset are better positioned to align ESG objectives with business goals, regulatory compliance, and market expectations. Integrated data systems offer a single source of truth for tracking emissions, resource use, diversity metrics, and ESG-linked financial products. Banks risk falling into fragmented reporting and inconsistent decision-making without such systems, ultimately weakening their credibility with regulators and stakeholders.

This integration, however, is not purely technical. It requires organizational alignment on data ownership, system interoperability, and reporting standards. The most compelling cases involved cross-functional teams collaborating to develop shared taxonomies and protocols, including IT, risk, compliance, and sustainability. These efforts often involved a phased approach, beginning with data mapping exercises and progressing toward real-time dashboards and automated ESG scoring tools. In some instances, banks used pilot projects to test new systems before rolling them out across the institution, which helped to build internal support and reduce implementation risks. Furthermore, digital tools such as AI-powered analytics and natural language processing are increasingly used to extract insights from unstructured data, enhance scenario modeling, and inform sustainability-linked credit and investment decisions. These technologies can expand ESG intelligence across the organization, but only if paired with strong governance, data literacy, and user adoption strategies. Banks that invested in training and change management alongside their digital upgrades reported higher internal engagement and more consistent application of ESG criteria in daily operations.

Data infrastructure is critical for operationalizing ESG goals. Bank A's development of a digital dashboard to track taxonomy alignment and emissions exemplifies how technology can enhance transparency and inform decision-making. Conversely, Bank C's reliance on spreadsheets created inconsistencies and undermined learning. ESG systems must be embedded into enterprise platforms, linked with risk and finance data, and governed by clear protocols to ensure consistency, ownership, and usability (Lozano, 2015; Eccles et al., 2014). In Bank B, adopting ESG data architecture allowed product teams to simulate the environmental impact of their offerings. Using these simulations, the sustainability team co-designed lending strategies that favored clients investing in renewable energy and small and medium-sized enterprises (SMEs) transitioning to greener operations. Such examples highlight how integrated data systems are not merely tools for compliance but strategic assets for innovation.

Cultural Alignment and Narrative Coherence

Cultural alignment is pivotal in determining whether organizations embrace or resist sustainability initiatives. It links formal systems to informal values, language, and norms. It ensures that sustainability is not only documented but also believed and enacted. Banks with values-based cultures used storytelling, internal campaigns, and rituals to build momentum. In contrast, where ESG was viewed as externally imposed or "not our job," even well-resourced efforts floundered. Leadership visibility and employee-led initiatives were key to bridging this gap. Even well-structured ESG strategies can fail to gain traction without a supportive culture. In the banks studied, successful integration of sustainability was closely linked to cultural values emphasizing openness, collaboration, and long-term thinking. Organizations with adaptive and learning-oriented cultures were likelier to translate sustainability goals into day-to-day behaviors. This cultural receptivity enabled ESG narratives to resonate more deeply, making sustainability a strategic imperative and a shared internal commitment. Banks that invested in fostering this alignment, through leadership communication, staff engagement, and storytelling, reported greater coherence between what was said and what was done (Aidanpää & Sjöberg, 2021).

Narratives serve as powerful tools for anchoring sustainability within institutional identity. Leaders who consistently framed sustainability as integral to the bank's mission, rather than an external requirement, were more successful in fostering internal coherence. These narratives helped staff understand the "why" behind ESG, linking it to core values such as trust, responsibility, and innovation. In contrast, when sustainability was communicated solely through compliance or reputational lenses, it remained peripheral and transactional. Symbolic acts, such as executive visibility in ESG events, including sustainability in internal awards, or featuring ESG champions in corporate communications, also reinforced narrative coherence. They signaled that sustainability mattered at every level, not just on paper. Such practices helped bridge the gap between aspiration and action, aligning informal culture with formal ESG objectives (Kohnke, 2017).

At the same time, resistance to cultural change continued to be a persistent challenge. Legacy norms, siloed departments, and short-term performance pressures sometimes clashed with sustainability priorities. In these instances, change agents played a crucial role. By initiating dialogue, highlighting internal success stories, and fostering cross-functional conversations, they contributed to a gradual cultural shift. Ultimately, cultural alignment and narrative coherence are not static achievements but dynamic processes. As one executive said, "You have to keep telling the story, especially when the strategy shifts or external expectations evolve." Sustainability becomes embedded in systems and mindsets when stories, symbols, and structures are aligned.

Capacity Building and Incentive Alignment

Building internal capacity is crucial for integrating sustainability into a bank's operational framework. Capacity and competence involve sustained investment in skills, roles, and training. Icelandic banks reported role overload and limited ESG career progression. Leading institutions have created ESG academies, rotational programs, and technical upskilling initiatives across all levels. Several banks emphasized the need for "hybrid profiles," staff who understand sustainability and banking operations. Without this, ESG remained isolated and overly dependent on a few individuals. ESG goals cannot be realized without employees who possess the necessary knowledge, skills, and motivation to act. Across the case studies, one consistent theme emerged: sustainability integration depends not only on top-level strategy but on investments in organizational learning, workforce development, and incentive structures that reinforce desired behaviors.

Training played a central role in this capacity-building effort. Leading institutions offered structured programs on ESG fundamentals, regulatory frameworks, and sector-specific sustainability risks. In some cases, sustainability training was embedded into onboarding, leadership development, and compliance courses. These efforts helped demystify ESG concepts and signaled their relevance to all roles, not just to sustainability specialists. As Overton et al. (2022) argue, data and technology alone are insufficient without knowledgeable staff who can interpret and act on them. Beyond training, performance management and incentives were critical enablers. Banks that linked sustainability metrics to individual and departmental performance reviews are generally found to have more substantial alignment between strategic goals and operational behavior. Some institutions are tying extended ESG targets to executive compensation or team-level bonuses and these mechanisms can translate broad institutional commitments into tangible motivations at the employee level (Kohnke, 2017).

However, incentive alignment required careful calibration. If framed too rigidly, performance metrics risked incentivizing short-term or superficial actions. Several interviewees emphasized the importance of qualitative feedback, narrative assessments, and learning-based evaluation in complementing quantitative targets. Capacity building thus went hand in hand with cultural change, encouraging curiosity, experimentation, and reflective thinking rather than compliance alone. Moreover, capacity extended beyond individuals to include teams, systems, and structures. Cross-functional ESG project teams served as learning laboratories where employees developed shared language, built relationships, and tested new tools. These projects also exposed capability gaps, particularly in data management, digital literacy, and stakeholder engagement, which informed broader training priorities. Finally, sustainability teams themselves required ongoing development. As the scope and complexity of ESG demands expanded, new skill sets were needed, including expertise in systems thinking, regulatory foresight, and digital innovation. Forward-looking banks supported their ESG staff with additional resources, peer learning, and external partnerships to remain at the forefront of evolving standards. These findings underscore that capacity building and incentive alignment are not secondary to ESG integration, they are its engine. By investing in people and creating meaningful reward structures, banks can foster more profound engagement, innovation, and accountability throughout the organization.

Project-Based Implementation and Learning Loops

Sustainability strategies are often broad and aspirational, but become real through concrete projects. Project-based implementation enables banks to operationalize ESG goals incrementally, test ideas in practice, and build internal legitimacy for broader transformation. Project-based implementation translates high-level goals into action. Banks used agile teams, pilot projects, and change management tools to advance sustainability. Embedding ESG into project management offices (PMOs) elevated visibility and coordination. One executive noted that "projects are where ESG lives or dies, it's where plans become decisions." Banks with strong PMO integration moved faster and more cohesively. The cases examined in this study demonstrate that successful sustainability efforts often start with small, targeted initiatives that are iteratively refined and scaled over time. These projects vary widely in scope from sustainable lending pilots to carbon footprint tracking, employee engagement campaigns, and green product innovations. What unites them is their capacity to generate learning. Rather than waiting for a perfect strategy, forward-thinking banks launch pilot projects to surface challenges early, adapt to evolving contexts, and develop institutional memory. As Hanelt et al. (2021) suggest, agile experimentation is a key enabler of organizational adaptability in dynamic sustainability environments.

Projects also serve as vehicles for cross-functional collaboration. By assembling teams from sustainability, risk, IT, compliance, and operations, banks create opportunities for knowledge exchange and collective problem-solving. These efforts not only build technical capabilities but foster trust, break down silos, and enhance alignment between strategic objectives and operational realities.

Importantly, project outcomes are not limited to deliverables; they also include insights, feedback, and reflections. Banks that embedded structured learning loops into their project processes, such as post-implementation reviews, stakeholder debriefings, and internal case documentation, were more effective in institutionalizing lessons learned. This continuous feedback mechanism helped refine future initiatives and gradually mature the bank's sustainability approach. Moreover, these projects can generate symbolic value. Visible successes demonstrate that change is possible, increase momentum, and help shift internal narratives from "why sustainability?" to "how can we do more?". In several banks, early wins, such as issuing a green bond or an energy efficiency audit, played a catalytic role in building support among skeptical teams or leaders. Nevertheless, project-based implementation must be strategically anchored. Projects risk becoming isolated experiments without clear links to broader ESG goals and governance structures. Successful institutions ensured that projects aligned with the bank's sustainability roadmap, contributed to key metrics, and were supported by senior sponsors who could champion their results and facilitate integration into core processes (AlNuaimi et al., 2022). Ultimately, this approach supports dynamic capability-building, the ability to sense opportunities, seize them through action, and transform routines based on experience. By treating sustainability implementation as an iterative learning process, banks achieve better outcomes and cultivate more resilient organizations.

9.2 Synthesis and Application

Together, the six components presented in this chapter, strategic alignment and executive mandate, distributed ownership with central coordination, integrated data systems and digital infrastructure, cultural alignment and narrative coherence, capacity building and incentive alignment, and project-based implementation with learning loops, form a comprehensive and dynamic framework for institutionalizing sustainability within banking organizations. This framework highlights that no single component can deliver meaningful change in isolation. Strategic alignment sets the direction and secures top-level commitment, but it must be activated through distributed ownership that empowers teams across the institution. That distributed responsibility, in turn, depends on a robust data infrastructure to ensure that efforts are transparent, measurable, and strategically coordinated. However, data and structures are insufficient without cultural alignment and shared values and narratives that make ESG ambitions resonate throughout the organization.

Capacity building and incentive alignment provide the mechanisms for sustaining engagement. They ensure that individuals are equipped with the proper knowledge and tools and motivated to integrate sustainability into their everyday decisions. Finally, project-based implementation and learning loops bring the entire framework to life. Organizations can translate abstract goals into practical applications through tangible initiatives, identify real-world constraints, and iterate toward improvement. The interplay among these components creates a system greater than the sum of its parts. The banks that succeeded in advancing ESG goals understood integration as a continuous, organization-wide journey, rather than a compliance obligation or a temporary campaign. They embedded ESG into governance, workflows, mindsets, and feedback mechanisms. Importantly, a mature sustainability architecture is not static. It is inherently adaptive and must be revisited regularly. External developments, such as new regulations, stakeholder expectations, or market disruptions, necessitate that institutions reassess and reconfigure their sustainability approaches. Internally, organizations must remain attuned to how their ESG efforts are perceived, implemented, and learned from. This framework invites reflection and dialogue. It can serve as both a diagnostic tool and a strategic roadmap. Banks can use it to identify strengths and gaps, align departments around shared priorities, and track their institutional development over time. Ultimately, the shift toward sustainability is not a destination but a transformation in how banks organize, act, and evolve.

9.3 Concluding Remarks

This chapter proposed a six-pillar framework for understanding and advancing the institutionalization of sustainability in banking. Drawing from Icelandic case studies and broader theory, it emphasized that ESG integration requires strategic clarity, cultural legitimacy, distributed responsibility, and operational tools. While each pillar is individually valuable, its impact is greatest when developed together. Misalignment, e.g., strong strategy but weak culture, can stall progress. Importantly, the framework is diagnostic as much as it is prescriptive. It helps banks assess where they are strong, vulnerable, and where to focus next. As sustainability expectations evolve, internal coherence will determine external credibility. The institutions that succeed will not treat sustainability as a department, but as a design principle for how they think, act, and lead. The chapter synthesizes the book's empirical and theoretical insights into six interdependent components that support institutional transformation. The core message is clear: sustainability must move beyond symbolic compliance or departmental siloing. It must become a way of thinking, organizing, and acting across the institution.

As banks face increasing regulatory demands, societal scrutiny, and climate-related risks, those that invest in their internal architecture, both structurally and culturally, will be best positioned to respond. Sustainability is not a trend to adopt. It is a new institutional logic to embody. The challenge now is not whether to integrate it, but how. Importantly, successful integration demands leadership at all levels of the institution. Executive mandates, middle-management alignment, and cross-functional collaboration are mutually reinforcing components of a governance system that supports sustainability from vision to execution. While senior executives shape strategic direction, the day-to-day translation of sustainability into action depends on the engagement of employees across all departments. This requires training, tools, and a profound cultural commitment that connects personal values with institutional purpose.

Furthermore, the chapter's findings indicate that progress hinges on dynamic capabilities, the ability to adapt, learn, and reconfigure. ESG priorities are evolving rapidly, and what is considered cutting-edge today may become the baseline tomorrow. To remain effective, banks must invest in feedback loops that ensure they listen to stakeholders, review outcomes, and adjust their strategies. Digital dashboards, internal audits, employee feedback mechanisms, and participatory forums all help ensure that sustainability governance remains a living system rather than a static blueprint. Integrating ESG principles is no longer a matter of external signaling, it is about building resilient, transparent, and forward-looking institutions. In this respect, governance is not just an enabler of sustainability, it is a test of it. Governance systems that can absorb complexity, facilitate dialogue, and create space for innovation are most likely to thrive in the face of escalating ESG expectations. Ultimately, the shift toward embedded sustainability is a strategic transformation. It touches every part of the organization, from leadership behaviors to IT systems, boardrooms, and branch networks. The banks that rise to this challenge will not only meet compliance thresholds but will shape the future of sustainable finance itself.

This chapter has proposed a holistic framework for embedding sustainability within banks' organizational structures and cultures. It synthesizes the book's empirical and theoretical insights into six interdependent components that support institutional transformation. The core message is clear: sustainability must move beyond symbolic compliance or departmental siloing. It must become a way of thinking, organizing, and acting across the institution. As banks face increasing regulatory demands, societal scrutiny, and climate-related risks, those that invest in their internal architecture structurally and culturally will be best positioned to respond. Sustainability is not a trend to adopt; it is a new institutional logic to embody. The challenge now is not whether to integrate it, but how.

References

Aidanpää, F., & Sjöberg, J. (2021). Cultivating sustainable narratives: Storytelling as a strategy for organizational change. *Journal of Organizational Change Management, 34*(4), 689–703.

AlNuaimi, B. K., Kumar Singh, S., Ren, S., & Budhwar, P. (2022). An integrated framework for implementing sustainable business practices in service organizations. *Business Strategy and the Environment, 31*(3), 1041–1055.

Carlsson, L., Matteby, J., & Söderlund, J. (2023). ESG coordination in practice: Exploring hybrid organizing in banks. *Sustainability Accounting, Management and Policy Journal, 14*(2), 298–316.

Eccles, R. G., Ioannou, I., & Serafeim, G. (2014). The impact of corporate sustainability on organizational processes and performance. *Management Science, 60*(11), 2835–2857. https://doi.org/10.1287/mnsc.2014.1984

Hanelt, A., Bohnsack, R., Marz, D., & Antunes Marante, C. (2021). A systematic review of the literature on digital transformation: Insights and implications for strategy and organizational change. *Journal of Management Studies, 58*(5), 1159–1197.

Kohnke, O. (2017). It's not just about technology: The people side of digital transformation. In M. Kreuzer (Ed.), *Digital transformation: A practitioner's guide* (pp. 57–75). Springer.

Lafioune, R., Desmarest, V., Poirier, I., & St-Jacques, M. (2023). Enabling ESG integration through distributed governance: The case of Canadian financial institutions. *Journal of Business Ethics*. Advance online publication. https://doi.org/10.1007/s10551-023-05469-6

Lozano, R. (2015). A holistic perspective on corporate sustainability drivers. *Corporate Social Responsibility and Environmental Management, 22*(1), 32–44. https://doi.org/10.1002/csr.1325

Overton, T., Larson, M., & Johnson, C. (2022). Building ESG capacity: Lessons from sustainability training programs. *Training & Development Journal, 76*(3), 54–61.

Tangi, L., Janssen, M., Benedetti, M., & Noci, G. (2020). Barriers and drivers of digital transformation in public organizations: Results from a survey in The Netherlands. *Government Information Quarterly, 37*(2), 101483.

9783032056368